HABITS
OF
SUCCESSFUL
PEOPLE

Habits of Successful People

Change Your Habits. Change Your Life.

Shawn Léon Nowotnik

am-biv-a-lent

For permission requests, please contact the publisher at: am-biv-a-lent.com.

Art direction, design, and layout by Shawn Léon Nowotnik. Proofreading and editing by Diane Busman.

This book is dedicated to my dad, Richard J. Nowotnik.

To those who are trying to change their life -

you can change your habits and thus change your life.

CONTENTS

PREFACE

Habits are powerful and completely within your control. In this book, you will discover the habits that have changed the lives of many of the most successful people in the world. These habits can change your life too. Although it would be impossible to identify every habit down to its minutia, I have identified the most common habits of successful people, offer why you need to incorporate them - and how to do just that.

How do I know these are the habits of successful people? I have spent the past 20 years asking many of the most successful people in the world what habits make them successful. Through one-on-one conversations with successful actors and actresses, athletes, authors, business leaders, comedians, creators, doctors, directors, musicians, producers, researchers, and titans of industry, I have compiled this amazing book of habits.

I also put these habits to the test!

Over the past two years, I have incorporated and lived the habits found right here in this book. I set out and successfully began to create positive habits using SMART goals (explained within this book). I worked on exercise, health, and nutrition, lost 20 pounds, decreased my cholesterol, and improved my sleep.

I reevaluated my communication style, became more emotionally intelligent, introduced breaks to recharge, began to partialize problems, and once again became solution focused. I worked on relationships, self-control, started therapy, and I learned to say no.

I learned you cannot change a habit by talking about it. No matter how long you say, "I'm going to change," it will mean little or nothing without action. And to be honest, once I began the process of creating a new habit, it was painless.

>**"You are what you do, not what you say you'll do."** Carl Jung

The fear of change is always worse than the reality of the task that lays before us. By the time my first new habit was automatic, I could not wait to start forming the next habit. This process continued throughout my journey of forming habits of successful people and still does to this day.

There's not a doubt in my mind that anyone who applies these habits will be successful. This book has nearly every habit you need to change your life. And, because I and so many others have been successful utilizing these habits, I absolutely know you will too! If you change your habits, you will change your life. I promise!

INTRODUCTION

We are a culmination of our habits. In time, our habits define us. When we brush our teeth in the morning (and at night), when we fasten our seatbelts upon entering a car, or when someone bites their fingernails when they're nervous, these actions are all habits that have been formed over time. Healthy habits strengthen our ability to lead successful lives. Unhealthy habits diminish our ability to succeed and can lead to our demise.

The old saying "You can't teach an old dog new tricks" could not be further from the truth. Everyone is capable of change. *EVERYONE!* We are resilient and adaptive creatures that with the right habits can and will change ourselves and the world around us. By eliminating unhealthy habits, we are able to achieve unbelievable feats and lead the lives we once only dared to dream of.

No matter how many successful habits you have in your arsenal, the habits offered in this book will provide you with opportunity for further growth. And if success is what you desire, then you're in the right place to learn and obtain the habits of the world's most successful people. Grab a pen and paper, prepare to take some notes, and start turning pages.

"You can't go back to yesterday, because you were a different person then."

Alice in Wonderland

Today is your day…

WHAT IS A HABIT?

A habit is an automatic response to a situation that has been encountered frequently in the past. Repetition of the behavior creates a mental association between the situation and the response, so that it becomes automatic (lacking thought) whenever the stimulus is encountered.

How powerful are habits? Every day about 40% of our actions are the result of habits. Therefore, we are the sum of our habits. It's important to understand that habits never go away. They are only replaced by more powerful habits. The great news is that you can change your habits for the better.

Habits are not formed or broken overnight. Habits become part of your psyche over a period of time where they become second nature to us. Habits are an evolutionary means to becoming more efficient as human beings. Turning everyday actions into habits frees up our brains for more important or life-preserving decisions.

Believe it or not, our brains are operating on autopilot for nearly half of all our actions. This is both a good and bad thing. From an efficiency point, it's incredible, but from the perspective of having a bad habit, it's disagreeable

7

and often harmful to us. Consequently, that's why we need to know how habits operate.

Habits are based on cues, cravings, routines, and rewards. They are continual feedback loops in our brains. Cues tell the brain which habits to use and when. Cravings are desires for something. Routine is an activity, emotion, or behavior. Rewards are the factors that your brain uses to determine whether or not a loop is valuable to you.

Habits are created by cue and reward. This results in cravings and reminds you to repeat behaviors. Therefore, if you wish to break a habit, you need to focus on changing the routine. If you are trying to break the habit of let's say - unhealthy snacking, a healthy routine will still provide a reward, or your brain would not be satisfied.

First, is the cue. What craving triggers the behavior? What were you feeling when you were triggered? What reward were you looking for? Is it an environmental trigger or internal? The more you know, the easier it will be to replace the negative or unproductive habit with a positive habit.

Second, people might crave different things based on different pieces of information, but in practice, they don't respond to the same cues. Cues become cravings when they are transformed into thoughts, feelings, and emotions of the observer.

Third, to promote healthy habits, you need to examine the routine or behavior you want to change. Ask, why do I have this routine? What do I benefit from doing this routine? What kind of satisfaction is received from repeating this routine?

Fourth, you need to evaluate the reward. What reward do I get from engaging in this habit? Is there an immediate gratification? Is it a distraction or way of avoiding another thing? By knowing the why, it will be easier to replace the negative habit with a positive habit that provides a reward.

Remember, there's a huge misconception that habits are broken by willpower. Nothing could be further from the truth. Willpower plays no role in breaking bad habits. You break bad habits by replacing the habit with a positive one that fulfills your reward loop.

HOW TO MAKE/BREAK HABITS

1). Start Small/Ask Why

We live in an era where many individuals expect instant gratification. Quite often, people confuse the fast-paced, fast food, social media world with the laws of nature (reality). Habits are not created in a day. Habits are created incrementally over a period of time. By making small but effective changes, a person can begin to build a sustainable habit, but you must start small. Rome wasn't built in a day. Again, you're looking for small incremental change, not instant change.

How do you start small? You start small by choosing a single habit you wish to add to your library of positive habits. Maybe, you want to begin the process of overcoming addiction. In order to pursue this habit, you need to ask yourself why you're pursuing this goal. The "WHY" is important because if you can't answer "WHY," how can you expect to know "WHY" you shouldn't give up and quit your new habit. The "WHY" allows you to fully commit and acknowledge that you're building this habit for the right reason (you).

2). Identify Barriers/Triggers

Developing good habits requires a clear understanding of all the triggers and barriers that are in your way. Underestimating your barriers is one of the quickest ways to become defeated and disheartened. Be aware that stressors often trigger past unhealthy habits. By having this awareness, you are better prepared to utilize a healthy coping skill.

What is a healthy coping skill? A healthy coping skill can be exercise, meditation, deep breathing, or even chewing gum instead of smoking. Anything that is healthy, alleviates stress, or is a healthy supplement rather than giving in to an unhealthy habit or giving up on a new habit is a healthy coping skill. Remember, it's important that you know your go-to coping skills to avoid triggering past unhealthy habits.

3). Create a Routine

In order to add a good habit to your life, the first thing you need to do is do it every day. That way, once you do it regularly, you will not only learn to do that habit more, but it will also become part of your daily routine. If you're trying to break an unhealthy habit, it's imperative you find something that is healthy to replace the unhealthy habit with. The more you enjoy the routine, the more likely it is you will succeed.

4). Commit to Your Change and Remain Positive

In order to achieve success, you must commit to practicing healthy habits. It's not as though you won't face obstacles or challenges from time to time. However, you must stay determined and manage each challenge with a positive attitude. It is vital to stay optimistic whenever you are trying to develop healthy habits in yourself. Positive thinking not only helps you to overcome negative feelings, but it also helps you to effectively handle problems associated with stress.

5). Ask for Help (friends and family)

The people closest to you have a huge impact on your habit change. Asking isn't easy for some people, but the payout of asking is huge. If you let your friends and family know about which habit you want to build, then they will most often be supportive and be able to help you see the habit through. Having your inner circle on your team is a plan for success.

6). Change Your Environment

Environment plays a crucial role in the success or failure of habit formation. Certainly, we can't always navigate around barriers and triggers, but when you change the environment, you are more likely to succeed. Remember, you're trying to manage risk and replace unhealthy environments with healthy ones that best serve your goals.

7). Celebrate Each Victory

As you celebrate small victories, you are more motivated to accomplish your new goal. It not only helps you to minimize the chance of falling back into the old habit, but it also encourages you to make a good habit a part of your life. The act of rewarding yourself for making progress stimulates the reward circuits in your brain, which create a sense of accomplishment and helps motivate you to continue.

8). Forgo All-or-Nothing Thinking

A person with all-or-nothing thinking tends to view life in extremes; he or she is either successful or unsuccessful. Relative to performance, you are either awesome or awful. If you're not perfect, then you're not a success. All-or-nothing thinking diminishes the positive things you accomplish as inconsequential or unworthy. Excluding the positive in this way is unfair to you and self-destructive because it leaves you feeling rejected and unappreciated.

9). Replace an Unhealthy Habit

It is easier to break an unhealthy habit by replacing it with a more desirable habit. You are substituting one habit for another, rather than solely trying to stop an undesirable habit. "Cold turkey" is not the best course of action when it comes to habits. The goal is to make the healthy habit repetitive and automatic, which then embeds the habit into memory.

10). Be Patient/Stay the Course

Habit forming is a long-term process. Be patient with yourself. It takes time and persistence to change habits. Changing habits isn't as easy as flipping on a light switch. It's more like turning a dial upward or downward. Be open to the process. Patience is key.

> **"If you know you are right, stay the course even though the whole world seems to be against you and everyone you know questions your judgment. When you prevail, and you eventually will if you stick to the job – they will all tell you that they knew all along you could do it."**
> Ralph Waldo Emerson

Everything worth doing takes time. Before you know it, you will have broken unhealthy habits and replaced them with healthy ones. Ultimately, by knowing your "WHY," you will achieve the successes you set out to accomplish. The question isn't, will you succeed? The question is, just how far will you go?

SUCCESSFUL PEOPLE DON'T

1). Blame Others

Successful people don't place blame on external factors (or other people) for their problems, as this gives those sources more power and drains their energy. It is impossible to take control of your life when you direct blame at others. When you stop blaming others, you are forced to take full responsibility, which helps you realize that you are in charge of your life and can direct it however you wish.

2). Catastrophize

Successful people don't catastrophize. What exactly is catastrophizing, you ask? Catastrophizing is a cognitive distortion that prompts people to jump to the worst possible conclusion, usually with very limited information or objective reason. When a situation is upsetting, but not necessarily catastrophic, they still feel like they are in the midst of a crisis. Successful people absorb a wide variety of pertinent information and remain calm, utilize their coping skills, and look for solutions.

3). Complain

The difference between successful and unsuccessful people is that the unsuccessful ones complain and don't do anything, while the successful ones shut their mouths, accept what's given to them, and take action. Instead of complaining, they try to improve their situation.

4). Look for Shortcuts

Successful people don't look for shortcuts or quick fixes. They develop habits based on what they learned from past failures as well as working harder than anyone else. They create systems that work for them consistently, rather than attempt to take shortcuts. Successful people put in the hard work and never give up.

5). Self-sabotage

Successful people do not self-sabotage. They realize self-sabotage is the act of choosing nonproductive ways in order to prevent painful feelings about oneself that one wants to avoid. It makes people feel less effective in their behavior, and it distorts their view of the world.

6). Act on Emotions

When it comes to making important decisions, successful people think before they act. They do not make rash or spontaneous emotional decisions. They do not react to a situation, but rather they respond to it. They take whatever time they deem necessary to evaluate the situation before coming up with a solution and acting upon it.

7). Wait for the Right Time

The world favors those who take imperfect action over those who wait until they have it all. Successful people understand there is no better moment than now to start the journey toward success and a fulfilling life. Again, they don't react emotionally. They respond with logic and reason. They create an action plan and then go for it.

"Don't wait. The time will never be just right."
Napoleon Hill

8). Pass on Opportunity to Learn

Successful people create or take opportunities to learn. When they don't know something, they admit it and rather than rely on others, they seek out to learn how to maintain their self-sufficiency. That being said, successful people know how to delegate and are aware they cannot know everything.

"Nothing is more expensive than a missed opportunity to learn." H. Jackson Brown, Jr.

TIME IT TAKES FOR A HABIT

Since I receive this question every week asking how quickly a person can establish a new habit, let me address it right away. According to a 2009 *European Journal of Social Psychology* study, it takes an average of 66 days for a new behavior to become automatic, but it can take as little as 18 days or as long as 264 days. Rather than focus on time, let's focus on the benefits of creating a new habit, not on how long it may take.

> **"Your net worth to the world is usually determined by what remains after your bad habits are subtracted from your good ones."**
> Benjamin Franklin

Additionally, breaking an unhealthy habit often takes longer than creating a healthy habit, and it's highly dependent on several factors, including who is undertaking the change, the length of time the habit has existed, personality and mindset, and whether the habit is precipitated by addiction, mental illness, trauma or other factors. On a positive note, all habits, including unhealthy habits, can be changed.

SMART GOALS

There's not a more universal way for an endeavor to fail than starting it without specific and measurable goals. How many talented individuals do you know that have shared brilliant and passionate ideas, but their plans never seem to come to fruition? Maybe you're one of those individuals. Ambition and talent are not enough. Without realistic and measurable goals, your idea is simply a dream.

"The difference between dreams and goals is a timeline and accountability." Dr. Phil

The idea that you can lose weight without a specific and measurable plan to change your diet; achieve wealth without a realistic understanding of finance; or improve your personal or professional life without a timely goal is a plan for failure! Without specific, measurable, achievable, relevant, and time-bound (SMART) goals, your likelihood of a successful outcome decreases exponentially. Conversely, with a SMART goal, the likelihood of your idea succeeding increases up to 33%.

SMART goals have been praised by many of the most successful athletes and sports teams, authors and creators, entrepreneurs and businesses, producers, and directors, educators, and organizers, and by spiritual and world leaders. SMART goals play a crucial role in the treatment of addictions, mental health, business development, entrepreneurship, education, career planning, and health and fitness. Anyone who has a goal can and should apply SMART goals.

> **"All successful people have a goal. No one can get anywhere unless he knows where he wants to go and what he wants to be or do."**
> Norman Vincent Peale

What is your goal? Whether you want to go from the copy room to the boardroom, the kitchen to owning a bakery, or from addiction to sobriety, SMART goals will get you there. Below is a step-by-step guide of how to turn your dream into a SMART goal. It's time for you to stop dreaming and start succeeding!

1). Specific (who, what, when, where, why).

>   **Who** is involved?
>
>   **What** do I want to accomplish, resources?
>
>   **When** is this goal due (time-bound also)?
>
>   **Where** will it happen, where is it located?
>
>   **Why** is this goal important to me?

Remember, you need to be able to clearly answer the who, what, when, where, and why in order for you to fulfill the specificity section of your SMART goal.

"You can't manage what you don't measure. What gets measured gets improved."
Peter F. Drucker

2). Measurable (how much, how many, how often).

SMART goals are determined in measurable units. The goal should be objective (units of measure, facts), not subjective (based on emotions). How much, how many, and how often are important questions to be answered in the measurable goal. Additionally, this stage necessitates how and when you will determine your goal is achieved.

3). Achievable (attainable, identify constraints, resources).

SMART goals need to be attainable within a specific timeframe. The goals may be challenging, but they should not be unattainable. In this stage, you must identify any constraints. If there are constraints, ask yourself how you will overcome them. This is when you determine if you possess the skills, experience, and credentials required for achieving this goal. If not, are there any preliminary steps you must take in order to begin this stage of your SMART goal? You may need resources to attain your goals, but you must maintain responsibility to ensure the goal is applicable, meaningful, resourced, and achieved.

4). Relevant (applicable, meaningful, the why).

This is the most important and overlooked question when pursuing a goal. You must ask yourself, does this goal matter to you and does it align, not only with your other goals, but with what accomplishing this goal will mean to you. Does this goal align with your belief system and long-term goals? This is often referred to as the "why" stage. Why am I doing what I do? Is what I'm doing applicable and meaningful? Is this a worthwhile pursuit? Is this the most appropriate time? Am I doing this for the right reasons? If you can't answer the "why," then it's time to reevaluate your goal.

5). Time-bound (time-limited, timely, evaluative).

What is the timeline for your goal? A timeline will provide you with motivation and accountability. If your goal is to obtain a new job, you may give yourself 90 days. This is also the stage where you evaluate if you haven't achieved your goal, why not. If you haven't achieved your goal, it's time to evaluate if your goal was unrealistic, or you may have run into unanticipated barricades on the way to accomplishing your goal.

EXERCISE AND HEALTH

There is an undeniable connection between exercise and success, which is why so many successful people, from titans of industry to entrepreneurs and celebrities, have discovered it. Without our health, we decrease our ability to succeed in life. Regular exercise strengthens your physical and mental state, which lifts up your whole being. Leaders are able to lead because they display excellence in a wide range of areas, including health and fitness. A person who is successful recognizes health as one of his or her most valuable commodities.

> **"I seriously doubt that I would have been as successful in my career (and happy in my personal life) if I hadn't always placed importance on my health and fitness."**
> Sir Richard Branson

Exercise has numerous benefits that keep successful people operating at optimum health. Below are a few:

1). Exercise reduces stress. Stress is a literal killer of dreams and our physical being. Have you ever been so stressed out that you have difficulty performing basic tasks? Among the reasons why successful people exercise regularly is because they know if they remain in stress all the time, they cannot deliver their best. Engaging in regular exercise at least 4 to 5 days a week not only helps you succeed, but it also helps you reduce the stresses associated with being a leader.

"Take care of your body. It's the only place you have to live." Jim Rohn

2). We have all read about moody geniuses, but their successes are far and few between compared to those who maintain a healthy mindset. Exercise is proven to improve mood and creativity. By exercising, various brain chemicals (endorphins) are stimulated, leading to feelings of happiness, relaxation, and less anxiety. Successful people understand that feeling good naturally leads to better focus and enhanced creativity. How can anyone expect to succeed when they have unhealthy levels of stress? Exercise is a step in the right direction for reducing or eliminating stress.

"I dwell in possibility." Emily Dickinson

3). Success is not a sprint. It's a marathon. Endurance is key. Successful people are known to work long hours. How can anyone maintain a demanding work schedule without endurance?

You can't! There's a reason many titans of industry get up early to exercise. Exercise improves your heart, lungs, and circulatory system, and brain function. It stimulates positive mood, endurance, and can delay or prevent many diseases - diseases that can disrupt a successful life.

"Come what may, all bad fortune is to be conquered by endurance." Virgil

4). Wars are won and lost due to sleep or lack thereof. Though you may not be in an active war zone, success has its share of battles. Battles that require endurance. How can you expect to have strength and endurance without proper sleep? Exercise improves sleep. You can fall asleep faster, sleep better, and deepen your sleep through diet and exercise.

The CDC advises that healthy adults need between 7 and 9 hours of sleep per night. Don't fall into the trap of saying you're "too busy" to get your sleep. With sufficient sleep, we improve our mental and physical health, reduce stress, and maintain our routines that are necessary for success. There's no sleep short cut!

When it's all said and done, it doesn't matter what form of exercise you do, whether it's cardio, weightlifting, yoga, or another activity. Exercising improves your health, well-being, emotional stability, productivity, and creative thinking. Successful people make time for exercise, and you should too!

NUTRITION

Successful people understand a healthy body and mind belong together. Successful people know that unhealthy food keeps them from achieving success. They know that they cannot sacrifice nutrition in order to achieve success. By eating a healthy diet, they can stay fit and energetic and achieve what they need to accomplish.

> **"Our food should be our medicine and our medicine should be our food."** Hippocrates

Successful people eat breakfast, as it keeps them from overeating later in the day. They drink lots of water, as it hydrates them and helps them maintain homeostasis. They eat small portions (often), as it keeps cortisol levels down. They pack their own lunch or choose healthy restaurants. They primarily eat unprocessed food and eat whole grains.

> **"Today more than 95% of all chronic disease is caused by food choice, toxic food ingredients, nutritional deficiencies, and lack of physical exercise."** Mike Adams

Successful people avoid snacking unless it's a cheat day, as snacks are often loaded with fat, sugar, and sodium. And they don't eat after dinner as it keeps their body's metabolism in a fat-burning state. Successful people eat at home, at work, while traveling, and out at restaurants.

Then how do successful people maintain such good nutrition?

First, they prioritize fruits, vegetables, whole grains, and milk products. They include proteins, including seafood, lean meats, poultry, eggs, legumes, soy products, and seeds and nuts. Their dietary choices are low in saturated fats, trans fats, cholesterol, sodium, and added sugars. Last, they stay within their calorie needs by avoiding unhealthy foods and snacks.

How to Maintain Healthy Choices:

1). In order to maintain the best nutrition choices, successful people plan ahead. They write out their grocery list and only make purchases based on their pre-planned meals for the week. Once they shop for the week, they will meal prep (prepare healthy portions for the next day or for the week). Again, they select foods that are high in nutrition and low in fats, sugars, and sodium.

2). Successful people who have limited time available to grocery shop for themselves will often utilize fresh-to-door meal services. There are countless meal services that will provide up to three meals per day fresh to your door, or they will ship you pre-prepped meals, including all ingredients, so you can prepare healthy meals at home without having to plan or shop at the grocery store yourself.

3). When out at work, out of town, or traveling on the road, successful people will locate restaurants prior to arriving in order to identify locations with the healthiest nutrition options. If there are limited options, successful people will choose the most nutritious or utilize that day as their "cheat day." Pizza anyone?

"Instead of focusing on all the reasons you can't do something, you need to focus on all the reasons you can do something." Matt McLeod

Nutrition is a critical part of every successful person's regiment. Make nutrition part of yours.

SLEEP

In the old days, actors, artists, and rock stars were known to stay up all night partying and going without adequate sleep, but today's creators are different. Today, successful people know the importance of sleeping enough, which is why they make getting a sufficient amount of sleep a daily habit.

Successful people have come to realize that in order to achieve success in life, it is essential to get enough sleep. In addition to sharpening your brain, sleep helps to improve your mood. Mood has a direct correlation to your ability to function and create.

Researchers are discovering more and more about the significance of sleep, and of the consequences of not getting enough, so there is more and more evidence to suggest that getting enough is as important as nutrition and exercise.

> **"There is a time for many words, and there is also a time for sleep."** Homer

It's not always easy to get enough sleep when you're successful and in high demand. Having trouble falling asleep can often be attributed to stress, which is why many successful people have developed routines to reduce anxiety before bed. The last thing you do before bed is likely to determine how well and how much sleep you will get the next day, as it is often what sets your mood and energy level for the day.

> **"I firmly believe that sleep and recovery are critical aspects of an effective and holistic training program."** Tom Brady

Strategies for sleep include reading, which successful people report helps them relax and go to bed inspired. Unplugging allows your brain to register you are done checking email and messages. It alerts your mind the day is over. Making a to do list or journaling before bed allows successful people to relax and unload what they need to do tomorrow. Spending time with family or a significant other again allows your mind to separate work from home time and puts a person in a relaxed mood.

> **"Sleep is the best meditation."** Dalai Lama

Many successful people go for a walk or do light exercise to unwind and decompress before bed. Mindful reflection helps end the day on a grateful and positive note. Meditation allows a person to get their body in synch with their breathing and allow their body to relax and calm down after a busy day. Successful people skip alcohol before bed. Though it can help you fall asleep, it is counterproductive in achieving quality sleep.

> **"Have courage for the great sorrows of life and patience for the small ones; and when you have laboriously accomplished your daily task, go to sleep in peace."** Victor Hugo

Make sure to give sleep the attention it deserves, since sleep is just as important as nutrition and exercise for your health. How many hours of sleep are you getting each night? What are the habits you are utilizing before you go to bed?

START EARLY

Getting up early is one of the habits of successful people. This helps them plan for the day ahead so that they can effectively accomplish their daily tasks. Successful people are also known for making their beds right away. Why? Making your bed early gives you an immediate feeling of accomplishment. It clears your mind and reduces stress, as a clutter-free home makes for a clutter-free mind. It's an easy habit to get into; and it is in unison with getting up early. I started it six months ago, and I haven't looked back. It's the first task I accomplish each morning.

> **"If you make your bed every morning. You will have accomplished the first task of the day. It will give you a small sense of pride. And it will encourage you to do another task. And another."** US Navy Admiral William H. McRaven

After making their bed, successful people make good use of their time by incorporating exercise, meditation, and planning their activities for the day. Many of the most successful people report answering their emails by 6am in the morning, so they can focus on more important issues when they get into the office.

Successful people cite the fact that it's easier to concentrate in the early hours when there are fewer distractions, as everyone else in your home is probably still asleep. You're less likely to receive texts and calls during that time as well.

Successful people report the early riser's schedule is more aligned with traditional business professionals, entrepreneurs, technology startups, athletes and traveling creative types. There seems to be a correlation between early risers being more proactive personality types, which may translate into better creative output.

> **"Some people dream of success, while other people get up every morning and make it happen."** Wayne Huizenga

What's most important is finding a schedule that fits your work routine and promotes a productive work style, is in synch with your sleep pattern, maximizes when your cognition is best (early morning or later in the morning), is conducive to your lifestyle, and allows you to still obtain your necessary and much needed sleep.

Ask Yourself: Am I an early riser? How early works best for me? How do I need to start my day in order to form the most productive morning habit?

FOCUSED THINKING

Focused thinking is when the brain uses its best ability to focus and ignore all unnecessary information. The prefrontal cortex of your brain plays an important role in this process, controlling your attention and memory, as well as helping you make decisions and solve problems. For around 30 minutes every day, successful people make it a habit to sit down and think about everything they need to know about a given subject matter. Then, they can analyze everything in a better way and better strategize how to achieve their goals.

> **"Concentrate all your thoughts upon the work at hand. The sun's rays do not burn until brought to a focus."** Alexander Graham Bell

When I'm in focused thinking mode, it's as though I have a one-track mind, and I can expeditiously break down a problem, write my next chapter, or knock out a steep climb. When utilizing focused thinking, it is important to be in a conducive environment and one that has few distractions. Remember, focused thinking should be done with music off. It takes brain power to listen to music, and it will distract from focused thought.

There's also a time for what is called diffused thinking. Diffused thinking is the opposite of focused thinking. It looks at the big picture and welcomes distractions. Thinking in the diffuse manner involves letting thoughts wander freely and making random connections. The diffuse mode of thinking does not happen in one particular part of the brain, but rather takes place throughout your brain.

Diffused thinking is the type of thinking that you do while jogging, hiking, sitting in a shop drinking your coffee, and it often leads to your brain forming a creative solution to a problem. Focused thinking is your brain processing very specific information deeply, whereas diffuse thinking involves analysis of very large amounts of information at once without going into great detail. Both have their place in your daily habits.

"When you visualize, then you materialize."
Denis Waitley

Neither focused nor diffused thinking is better than the other, as they are two sides of the same coin. Both are necessary to solve complex problems, create new innovations, and master a topic. What's important is that you make a concentrated effort to include focused and diffused thinking as part of your daily habit.

NETWORK WITH LIKE MINDS

The most connected people in the world are the most successful. When you network with like minds, you are more likely to succeed. The value of networking lies in the ability to develop and improve your skill set, stay current with trends in your industry, meet potential mentors, partners, and clients, and gain access to the necessary resources to fuel your career development.

It's important to remain diligent and only network with positive individuals. The company of other positive people who are successful will have a significant impact on your own success. That's why successful people prefer to form relationships with positive and motivated people. Since successful people believe exposure to negative people can negatively impact their personalities, they try to limit their contact with them regardless of what they may have to offer. Negativity breeds negativity.

In my experience, I know I can literally feel the presence of positive and negative people. There are the positive people you meet and instantly know they're going to be a valued friend or associate. Meanwhile, you've probably also experienced the type of person who casts a shadow over the room. If you want to succeed, make it a habit to surround yourself with like minds and avoid those that will drain you with negativity.

> **"Networking is a lot like nutrition and fitness: we know what to do, the hard part is making it a top priority."** Herminia Ibarra

Investing in your personal and professional relationships can pay dividends throughout your career, but how do you improve your network?

Utilizing social media to find like-minded individuals is a good start. It's one of the best uses of social media. It's also a great way to meet a large group of people who are also building careers like you. Additionally, there's a sense of universality, where you're not the only one who is building a network. Through the process, you make connections and build your ego strength as you realize you are not alone in the journey of success.

> **"Your network is your net worth."** Porter Gale

Decades ago, if you were a writer, you'd frequent a local watering hole, but today, successful people attend seminars, public speaking events, and self-improvement workshops to meet like-minded people. That's not to say the next Hemingway isn't sitting in your local bar, but odds are that you will meet many more people to network with at a business or self-help event.

I'm sure it doesn't take a lot of time to come to the realization that a TED Talk type event is a great place to meet other up-and-coming or established, talented, and like-minded people. Rather than attending an event as a consumer, consider speaking at an event where you can shine in front of an audience, and people will approach you wanting to network with you. Regardless of whether you speak at an event or not, even the shyest individual can meet a dozen like-minded people at an event.

> **"Networking is not about just connecting people. It's about connecting people with people, people with ideas, and people with opportunities."** Michele Jennae

Personal growth should continue to be part of your career trajectory. Networking alone will do little good if you stagnate and become dusty. Remember, like-minded attracts like-minded. Continue to be the person that asks questions, compliments others on their solutions, continues to read and research, pushes boundaries, and continues to flip problems on their head. Be the best version of you, and you will attract the best minds around.

How powerful is networking? When I started out in Hollywood in 1997, I didn't know a soul. In order to pay my bills, I was working as a welder Monday through Friday in Chicago and flying out to Los Angeles on the weekends. With my business partner, we began to pitch one of the first online talent agencies via hotel bars.

We would stay at the cheapest hotels in Los Angeles, but hang out at the Beverly Hills Hotel, Sofitel, Four Seasons, Standard, and the watering holes of the most successful people in Hollywood, such as Chasen's and Spago. These were places where we could network, ask questions, and share our passion with like-minded and talented people.

Within one weekend, I had walked the red carpet and attended the Golden Globe Awards, attended parties for Paramount Pictures, Universal Pictures, Warner Bros., Miramax, and many others. And I came home with dozens of business contacts.

Within a year of doing this, I was building our talent agency: producing indie films, working on record album art, and becoming someone others sought out to network with as I had a powerful inner circle of dozens of movers and shakers in Hollywood. Not just celebrities, but the true gears of the machine (agents, producers, assistants, party planners, and more).

You cannot succeed without networking. You need an audience who is eager for your product and service. You need people to desire what you possess and where they feel you have inherent value, even if it is to only to pick your brain within their trusted social network.

I cannot tell you enough about how valuable it is to simply be in earshot of the most talented people in the world. You learn about everyone and everything within their world. Networking is acquiring untold knowledge you cannot learn in books or via the Internet.

Networking will improve your skill set, keep you current with trends, allow you to meet potential mentors, partners, and gain invaluable resources. Remember to surround yourself with positive people and avoid the negativity of others.

In order to meet new people, utilize social media, self-help and creative seminars and business symposiums, frequent the watering holes of your target social network, and remember to continue to grow in order to be of value to yourself and others.

Last, don't let fear keep you from introducing yourself to others. You're not only helping yourself, but you're giving them a great opportunity to make you part of their social network. You bring with you a vast array of knowledge. How extensive is your social network?

MONEY ISN'T EVERYTHING

Quite often people believe success is only measured in monetary value. They work hard to find ways to make money and believe that becoming financially wealthy will make them successful. But successful people know getting rich is not a true measure of success because there are many other aspects that must be taken into account. Not everything that has value can be measured. Successful people report that rather than chasing after accolades from others or having a large bank account, they make it a habit to remind themselves that success is internal feeling of purpose and fulfilment.

> **"Success is not the key to happiness. Happiness is the key to success. If you love what you are doing, you will be successful."** Albert Schweitzer

Success is more than enjoying the journey. Success is the ability to be on the journey and continue on one's own path. Therefore, successful people know true success transcends wealth, popularity, external factors and is an internal value that cannot be compared to others. Using external measures of success as a guide means we are evaluating ourselves against standards set by someone else.

"Try not to become a man of success. Rather become a man of value." Albert Einstein

Thus, external measures are flawed because they were created by someone else. Therefore, we should not compare ourselves with external measures of success. I believe success is measured on uniquely different rulers, and each person has a different measuring stick as to what success is.

What Success Looks Like to a Successful Person:

1). Your work has a purpose, and you are passionate about what you do.

2). The achievements you have made so far are something you are proud of.

3). As you make others' lives better, you contribute to something bigger than yourself.

4). You are surrounded by people who care about you, and you care about them.

5). You are improving and evolving.

You owe it to yourself to make it a habit to measure your own success using your own ruler!

SELF-CONTROL

Do you find yourself playing hours of video games? Are you flipping through countless social media posts? Have you been *Keeping Up with the Kardashians*? Successful people refrain from such activities. Having self-control is key to improving your focus and decision-making ability. Successful people understand very well that self-control impacts their success exponentially.

> **"In that power of self-control lies the seed of eternal freedom."** Paramahansa Yogananda

Most successful individuals dedicate limited time to the things they find tempting but make no positive contribution to their success. I'm not suggesting you can't have fun, but it needs to be limited and utilized as a break, not as an unhealthy habit or a way of life.

> **"I count him braver who overcomes his desires than him who conquers his enemies; for the hardest victory is over self."** Aristotle

How to Improve Self-Control:

1). Remove temptation rather than trying to resist it. It is easier to manage environment or remove yourself from it than simply trying to white-knuckle through.

2). Monitor your self-control or lack thereof. By monitoring, you have a clear idea of your habits.

3). Stress is a major influence on loss of self-control. Manage your stress, and you will begin to more readily manage your self-control.

4). Show compassion to yourself. Failure is not permanent. If you lose self-control, regain composure, and start again, noting what you can do differently next time.

"Self-control is a key factor in achieving success. We can't control everything in life, but we can definitely control ourselves."
Jan McKingley Hilado

Self-control is 100% within your power, and once you master control over it, you will have more time than you ever imagined. What are you going to do with your newfound time?

COMMUNICATION

In order to be considered among the list of highly successful people, it is necessary to have excellent communication skills. In order for communication to be successful, both parties need to understand each other's messages and perspectives. Being able to understand others' perspectives not only makes you more empathetic, but also makes you easier to understand.

> **"The way we communicate with others and with ourselves ultimately determines the quality of our lives."** Tony Robbins

In order to be a successful communicator, you need to have the following habits mastered:

1). Be considerate. Do not monopolize the conversation and do ask others what their thoughts are on the topic of discussion. Remember, it's a discussion. Not a monologue. Also, don't interrupt the other person.

2). Be attentive to the speaker. Never utilize your phone or allow yourself to be distracted by what's going on around you.

3). Read your audience. Pay attention to non-verbal cues. Remember, between 70-90% of communication is non-verbal. Pay attention to your own body language and how it may be perceived.

"The most important thing in communication is to hear what isn't being said." Peter Drucker

4). Utilize reflective listening (repeating back what another says). Reflective listening allows the other person to clarify their points, ensuring that you both understand each other.

5). Stay on point. If you or the other person lose focus, if the conversation veers off, or tempers flare, take a moment to regain composure and offer to continue the conversation at another time when you both can focus on key issues.

Communication is how we transfer information. It is essential that you use it clearly and effectively, not only sharing your message, but also definitively understanding others. Nothing is more important than how we share information.

SOLUTION FOCUSED

It is all too common for us to focus on the negative aspects of a problem. More often than not, we repeat the same patterns of behavior that didn't work until negativity sets in. Negativity tends to cause people to focus on more problems instead of finding ways to resolve the problem and grow from it.

Identify your problems but give your power and energy to solutions.

Successful people focus on solutions rather than mere reactions and make a list of possible solutions instead of reacting to the situation. They don't react but instead take some time to analyze the situation completely. Successful people know that there is a solution to be found and are willing to focus on finding it.

"I never worry about the problem. I worry about the solution." Shaquille O'Neal

Though they do not initially want a problem to happen, they understand that it is an opportunity for growth, not a time to bury their head in the sand. They understand that by focusing on the problem, they wind up with more problems, whereas their focus on solutions promotes further solutions.

Steps to take to find solutions:

1). Identify the problem/s. Separate your emotions from the problem and identify fact from emotions.

2). Identify how you solved similar problems in the past and use this time to further come up with solutions.

3). Recognize what skills you have or will need to solve the problem.

4). Locate and utilize resources when the problem requires assistance.

5). Break the cycle. Change what didn't work and stop doing what doesn't work.

6). Decide which solution is best.

7). Develop a series of steps that will help you solve the problem.

8). Activate the solution.

9). Review results and adapt if changes are still needed.

"Great leaders are almost always great simplifiers, who can cut through argument, debate, and doubt, to offer a solution everybody can understand." Colin Powell

Solution-focused thinking requires letting go of negative thought patterns, which are often faced when confronted with problems. It requires recognizing what has worked in the past and asking hard questions, embracing collaboration, and reaching out to experts for guidance.

"Visionary people face the same problems everyone else faces; but rather than get paralyzed by their problems, visionaries immediately commit themselves to finding a solution." Bill Hybels

Solution-focused thinking follows logical steps, separating emotion out of the process and allowing successful people to come to the best resolution possible, while avoiding the pitfalls of self-pity and fearing the sky is falling. Successful people are always solution-focused, and you should be too. What problem will you focus on next?

DEPRIORITIZE/SAY NO

It's important to recognize that there are many tasks you should be removing from your list that don't add much value to your main goal. Most successful people know this, and they make it a habit to deprioritize these tasks because they know wasting time on unnecessary tasks will prevent them from attaining their goals.

> **"You have to decide what your highest priorities are and have the courage pleasantly, smilingly, and non-apologetically – to say no to other things."** Stephen Covey

Successful people make it a habit to give themselves a few moments before saying yes to anything. They use this time to ask questions, determine how long a task may take, and to evaluate if they can actually accommodate the time required for the request. Successful people want to address the tasks that will make the biggest impact, not those that will simply keep them busy.

> **"I'm actually as proud of the things we haven't done as the things I have done. Innovation is saying no to 1,000 things."** Steve Jobs

Successful people have learned to say no. It can be uncomfortable at first to say no, and it may seem easier to say yes, or to say you will think about it. But if the request doesn't suit your goal or needs - it's best to say no.

Furthermore, if you say you'll think about it, you open the door to be asked where you stand on the request once again. Moreover, successful people say no in order to be able to say yes to important things that are meaningful and that will allow them to maintain their success, in life, business, and other areas that drive their passion.

> **"The difference between successful people and really successful people is that really successful people say no to almost everything."**
> Warren Buffett

Remember, it can take a long time to earn the right to say no to almost everything. The first time you start a business, you often have to say yes to almost everything simply to establish how you function and learn what opportunities are available. That's how you determine where and how you can have the greatest impact and provide the best product or service.

That being said, remember you have the right and responsibility to use the power of no!

DAILY ROUTINES/STRUCTURE

You cannot achieve success by simply creating daily routines. People who are highly successful invest time creating these routines, but they also place equal value on following them. By making it a habit to follow routine, successful people continually better themselves. In addition to bettering themself, maintaining a positive daily routine comes with additional benefits, such as giving them structure, creating forward-moving habits, and creating momentum that will carry them through each day.

Benefits of daily routines and structure:

1). Reduce stress: Routines help stress levels fall. With a plan in place, you will feel more in control. Since all your important decisions will be made in advance, you can then focus on making good choices regarding the remaining ones.

2). Better health: Preparing everything from grocery shopping to meal prep and plans, from exercise schedules to sleep schedule, your health will be maximized. A healthier body makes for a healthier mind and a more successful person.

3). Psychological benefit: There's also a psychological benefit from having routines. Research has shown that routine can help alleviate anxiety, depression, stress, bipolar disorder, ADHD, and insomnia, among other conditions.

4). Quality of life: Having a routine assists with time management allowing more time to spend with friends and family, and more time to pursue other interests that are fun. Moreover, routines allow you to make time every single day to devote to your passion.

"A champion doesn't become a champion in the ring, he's merely recognized in the ring. His 'becoming' happens during his daily routine."
Joe Louis

Successful people take time to track their progress and reward themselves. Make sure you track via a journal, application, or via a to do list, and remember to reward yourself as it helps reinforce and support your goals. How are you going to track and reward yourself?

PARTIALIZING

Have you ever been overwhelmed by the depth and complexity of a task or problem? Do you ever forgo attempting a task or problem because it seems "too big" to attack? You're not alone. Many people avoid or fail to follow through with a task or problem because they are overwhelmed. So, how do you solve this issue? You learn to partialize your task or problem.

Successful people are outstanding at partializing tasks or problems. Partializing is when a person focuses on a part rather than the whole of a task. Successful people understand that there are incremental steps to solving complex problems. By partializing, people are much more successful at accomplishing tasks or solving complex problems.

> **"Divide each difficulty into as many parts as is feasible and necessary to resolve it."**
> René Descartes

How do successful people tackle problems? Successful people set goals and create a plan that ensures that the right action and steps are taken to reach the desired goal. Partializing is that way.

How to Partialize Step by Step:

1). Explore your thoughts and feelings about the task, and welcome exploration by anyone involved in the task.

2). Make a list of your strengths, not your weaknesses. Draw upon these strengths.

3). Elicit facts, ideas, and potential steps for a resolution.

4). Assess all the information and formulate a timely step-by-step plan.

5). Take action on the first step.

6). Evaluate and review the outcome of the step.

7). Adjust if you fail to accomplish a step.

8). Repeat the process on each subsequent step until the task or problem is completed.

Giving up is the most painful and unfulfilling way of not addressing a problem.

An example of partializing is depicted in the movie *What About Bob?* Richard Dreyfuss portrays Dr. Leo Marvin, and Bill Murray portrays a multi-phobic personality in a constant state of panic named Bob Wiley. In the movie,

Bob expresses to Dr. Marvin that he can't muster the ability to get home from the doctor's office due to his overwhelming phobias.

Dr. Marvin explains to Bob: "Don't think about everything you have to do in order to get out of the building," instead, "just think about what you must do to get out of this room, and when you get to the hall, worry about the hall" and so on.

Dr. Marvin refers to this as "*Baby Steps* (setting small reasonable goals)." Even though the movie is an over-the-top comedy, the idea of partializing is spot on.

Remember partializing is more concerned with addressing each part until you solve the whole. It's not about avoiding the big problem; it's about managing it step-by-step. Partialize the first part of the problem and before you know it your problem will be solved. Do you utilize partializing when taking on tasks or problems?

GRATITUDE

The most successful people engage in a simple, daily habit that helps them achieve more, be happier, and make a difference - and that is practicing gratitude. What is gratitude? Gratitude is a readiness to express appreciation and reciprocate kindness for what one has and for the opportunities that lay ahead. Simply, gratitude is being thankful for what one has and acknowledging future possibilities.

> **"Gratitude bestows reverence, allowing us to encounter everyday epiphanies, those transcendent moments of awe that change forever how we experience life and the world."**
> John Milton

People who are grateful see the bright side in even the darkest of circumstances. Rather than being discouraged by adversity, they are invigorated by the opportunity they have been given to step into the unknown and make their mark. Successful people practice the habit of being present.

> **"Gratitude is the healthiest of all human emotions. The more you express gratitude for**

what you have, the more likely you will have even more to express gratitude for." Zig Ziglar

By remaining in the present, we are able to maximize the benefits of every opportunity, and we can concentrate on the present instead of worrying about the past and the future. Gratitude is about the here and now, which is where successful people live. Focusing on the past or the distant future is where anxiety resides.

"Enjoy the little things, for one day you may look back and realize they were the big things." Robert Brault

Why should you live with gratitude? Gratitude powers the grateful. It promotes happiness. It unites people and brings us closer together, and it improves both mind and body health. Moreover, positive feelings such as gratitude and optimism counteract negative feelings such as envy, greed, and self-pity.

How do you practice gratitude? Spend time each day affirming the good things you receive and acknowledging in your mind - or via a journal - the ways in which others contribute to the quality and good in your life. What are you grateful for, and how do you acknowledge it?

MEDITATION

It seems you cannot listen to an interview or podcast today without a successful person, especially an actor, musician or business titan, who does not credit their use of meditation as a key ingredient in their success. Successful people express how meditation has added calm to their chaotic schedules and lives. Meditation is touted as a must have habit for many.

> **"Meditation is all about the pursuit of nothingness. It's like the ultimate rest. It's better than the best sleep you've ever had. It's a quieting of the mind. It sharpens everything, especially your appreciation of your surroundings. It keeps life fresh."** Hugh Jackman

Mediation has been noted to have played a vital role in the success and longevity of many people who have achieved success in life. Meditation is believed to have a myriad of benefits. Meditation's benefits include controlling stress, reducing anxiety, promoting emotional health, increasing self-awareness, lengthening attention span, aiding in preventing memory loss, helping fight addictions, improving sleep, and reducing pain.

What is meditation? Meditation can take many forms, but nearly all include four essential components: a quiet location with few distractions, a comfortable posture (sit, stand, lay), a focus of attention on breath, word, or an object, and an open and non-judgmental attitude (letting distractions pass without judging them).

How to Meditate:

1). Take a seat somewhere calm and quiet.

2). Set a time limit (5-10 minutes).

3). Notice your body.

4). Feel your breath as it goes in and out.

5). Notice when your mind has wandered and return your attention to the breath.

6). Don't judge yourself if your mind wanders. Simply refocus again on your breath.

7). Close with kindness (notice your body, thoughts, and emotions).

8). Slowly become aware of your environment.

9). Repeat daily.

"Meditation really improves my mental health and reminds me it's important to stay calm so I can feel safe in my body. We are all one body, and the calmer we are, and the more we find inner peace, the more the world will too."
Lady Gaga

Meditation takes practice, but once you are able to slow your mind, the benefits are amazing. As with any other skill, you have to practice it consistently until it becomes habitual. Think of it as exercising a muscle that you haven't exercised before.

As you train in mindful meditation, you gain a healthy perspective. You don't try to numb yourself of your thoughts and feelings. You learn to observe them, and in time, you may also start to understand them better. Where is your calm and quiet place going to be?

HUMILITY

We've all seen the flashy and over the top business leaders and celebrities, but most successful people are in the habit of being humble. Steven Spielberg, Sir Richard Branson, Quincy Jones, and Steve Wozniak are among some of the humblest people to grace the business world and entertainment industry. Why is it that so many successful people are humble?

"Humility is not thinking less of yourself; it's thinking of yourself less." C. S. Lewis

Successful people are humble because they are confident enough in their skills that they don't have to resort to boasting, bragging, or showboating. Moreover, successful people are known to correct their mistakes without argument, and they accept their shortcomings easily and without passing responsibility. Humble people own their actions whether they are great or abysmal.

"There is beauty and humility in imperfection."
Guillermo del Toro

A habit that sets successful people apart from everyone else is that successful people are happy learning from others. They listen to what others have to say and what others have to offer, including feedback. Successful people believe others have inherit value and learning from others will enable them to further succeed in life.

> **"We learned about gratitude and humility - that so many people had a hand in our success, from the teachers who inspired us to the janitors who kept our school clean... and we were taught to value everyone's contribution."** Michelle Obama

Don't confuse the habit of humility with low self-esteem, as it's quite the opposite. Humble people often have very healthy self-esteem. So much so, that they don't require external confirmation. Humility can be one of the most challenging habits of successful people often due to their prestigious position and fame.

> **"I tell my kids and I tell proteges, always have humility when you create and grace when you succeed, because it's not about you. As soon as you accept that, you can do it forever."**
> Quincy Jones

A few years back, I had the wonderful opportunity to speak with Sir Richard Branson at a private event honoring Sir Paul McCartney. I was walking the red carpet, and at the end of the carpet, I literally came inches away from walking right into Sir Richard. I excused myself and Sir Richard said "Please, excuse me." I said, "Sir

Richard, while we're having this moment, I have to tell you that today I flew your airline (Virgin) for the first time," and I pulled out my boarding pass.

Sir Richard immediately thanked me and asked how I enjoyed my experience. I went into great detail telling him how much I enjoyed it. So much so, that I admitted it was the best experience I've had in over a hundred flights to Los Angeles. I thanked him for the impact he had on his employees as I explained to him that their passion was a reflection of his. He expressed his gratitude.

What sets successful people like Sir Richard apart from others is he genuinely made me feel he was fully engaged, and that I was acknowledged. Not once did he assert his own importance, but rather kept the focus on me and his employees who made my experience amazing. My introduction to Sir Richard was a master class on humility that I will never forget.

Genuine humility is not thinking less of oneself, rather doing the opposite. Humility is an act of self-awareness, sensitivity, and kindness, which encourages candidacy, compassion, and benevolence. Humble leaders are aware of both their strengths and limitations. Always remember to be humble.

ACCEPT CHALLENGES

Everyone faces challenges in their lives but overcoming them is normal in the life of a successful person. Successful people make it a habit to accept that accidents happen, delays arise, problems are inevitable, and at times, things do not turn out exactly as they had planned.

"Our ability to handle life's challenges is a measure of our strength of character." Les Brown

What separates successful people from the average person is that successful people accept everyday challenges. They have the courage to handle unexpected situations. They accomplish things other people will not achieve because they do not accept challenges based on negativity or the fear of failure.

"We choose to go to the Moon in this decade and do the other things, not because they are easy, but because they are hard."
John F. Kennedy

Successful people don't shy away from pressure. In fact, they make it a habit to ask for the ball as the clock winds down. They accept the difficult assignments that others pass on, and they face obstacles and ambiguity with enthusiasm.

"Everything negative - pressure, challenges - is all an opportunity for me to rise." Kobe Bryant

Successful people:

1). Accept challenges with enthusiasm
2). Make a plan
3). Accept assistance if needed
4). Believe challenges are learning opportunities
5). Maintain a positive mindset
6). Never give up
7). Finish what they start

"It's lack of faith that makes people afraid of meeting challenges, and I believed in myself." Muhammad Ali

Successful people know their outcome in life is based on mindset. Therefore, they make it a habit to live with the mindset that the past cannot be changed and anxiety will not change the future in their favor. They conquer fear, rise to challenges, and are enthusiastic participants. Are you prepared to make accepting challenges one of your habits?

AUTHENTIC SELF

A successful person who is living their true authentic self is someone whose words and actions align. A successful person's authentic self goes beyond what they do for a living, level of fame, what they own, or who they are to others (boss, brother, girlfriend). It comes down to who they are at their core as a person. By living their dream career and dream life, successful people are living their authentic self.

How do you know if you're living your authentic self?

1). Take inventory by asking these questions: What are your core values? Are you living your core values? What activities make you feel alive? Do the people in your life make you happy or angry - or are they toxic? When you feel most alive and authentic, what are you doing, and who are you doing it with?

When it comes to living an authentic life, successful people make it a habit to prioritize the people and activities that bring them joy and meaning.

2). Be present: Successful people realize that authenticity depends on their ability to be present with themselves, no matter what is happening around them. You can't be authentic if you're distracted by your thoughts or reacting to external events. Being aware of your actions and expressing yourself fully will allow you to take actions that feel more authentic to your true self.

Remember, do not be concerned about how you appear to others, whether you meet their approval, or what you should do next. Instead, reflect within and on your values.

3). Social circle: Successful people are sure to periodically assess their social circles. They make sure to be surrounded by people who support and encourage them. A supportive social circle will make you shine as your authentic self.

You need authentic people in your life if you want to live an authentic life.

4). Speak the truth: By practicing an openly assertive communication style, you foster open, honest exchange while also considering the needs of others. This results in balanced conversations where both parties benefit.

5). Take action toward authenticity: Successful people realize that every action they make each and every day adds up to who they are as an authentic person. They make sure to move forward with their goals and involve themselves in activities that bring them happiness.

You must make sure you are not succumbing to others' dreams and goals and losing focus on your authentic needs.

6). Perspective: Successful people know that at times they need to step back and see the bigger picture. At times, a person may even need to remove themselves from the situation to better understand what's going on.

Reflection is essential.

7). Recognize internal vs. external: Successful people are able to determine if a source of motivation is internal or external. Internal factors are rooted in a person's being or authentic self, where external influences may be money, status, recognition, or people.

Ask yourself, am I living as my authentic self?

EMOTIONAL INTELLIGENCE

Successful people are individuals with a high emotional intelligence (EQ) and are able to identify and control their emotions as well as understand the emotions of others. Having high EQ helps successful people build relationships, reduce associates' stress, defuse conflict, and establish career satisfaction. Emotional intelligence affects career and schoolwork, physical health, mental health, and relationships. Many employers rate having a high EQ as a primary reason for hiring a new employee.

High EQ includes the following five elements:

Self-Awareness: Having self-awareness means being able to recognize one's feelings, emotional triggers, strengths, weaknesses, motivations, values, and goals, and be able to understand how they influence the way one thinks and acts.

"The curious paradox is that when I accept myself just as I am, then I can change."
Carl R. Rogers

Self-Management: The ability to manage emotions is the ability to control feelings of anger, anxiety, stress, and bad moods. Everyone, even those with a high EQ, experiences these feelings, but the key to self-management is to control them rather than allow them to control you. Those with strong self-management are able to delay responding brashly to stressful or negative situations. They are able to remain level-headed and respond rather than react.

"It isn't stress that makes us fall--it's how we respond to stressful events." Wayde Goodall

Social Awareness: In order to be socially aware, one must be able to recognize and interpret non-verbal cues. Non-verbal cues tell the recipient how someone else is feeling or thinking, and it allows you to recognize their emotional state of change as the conversation develops.

Empathy: Social awareness includes empathy. Empathy is the capacity for connecting with others on an emotional level and taking into account their feelings, concerns, and viewpoints. This skill is crucial for negotiating with internal and external stakeholders, as it helps you anticipate and understand what they need.

"When dealing with people, remember you are not dealing with creatures of logic, but with creatures of emotion." Dale Carnegie

Relationship Management: The ability to develop and maintain relationships, create positive connections with others, communicate clearly and efficiently, influence and inspire others, function well in a group, understand humor, and manage conflict are essential to relationship management.

"Before you are a leader, success is all about growing yourself. When you become a leader, success is all about growing others." Jack Welch

People with high EQ can manage their emotions and therefore are much more able to manage stress. Moreover, because successful people can manage their stress, they tend to have positive mental health. By having high EQ, successful people are better communicators and are able to engage more effectively, thus expressing their emotions and building healthier relationships. Do you have high emotional intelligence?

"It takes something more than intelligence to act intelligently." Fyodor Dostoyevsky

JOURNALING

Successful people know that journaling is a productive habit. Though they journal at various times throughout the day, many successful people report that journaling in the morning allows them to start their day with clarity. Journaling can also be utilized for tracking food, fitness, gratitude, for sketches, and for to do lists. There is no right or wrong way to journal.

Benefits of Journaling:

1). Achieve goals: It is easier to keep track of your intentions if you write your goals down in a journal. Maintaining accountability will help you stay on track and remind you how to achieve the goals you've set.

"It is not only what we do, but also what we do not do, for which we are accountable." Moliere

2). Track your progress: Rereading previous entries will help you gauge how much progress you have made over time.

Small progress is still progress.

3). Gain self-confidence: You will boost your confidence when you see your daily, weekly, monthly, or yearly progress. There's nothing better than seeing your pattern of success written out in front of you.

"As soon as you trust yourself, you will know how to live." Johann Wolfgang von Goethe

4). Improve your writing: You practice the art of writing when you keep a journal every day. It will also help improve your overall communication skills if you keep a journal for expressing your thoughts and ideas.

"In the journal I do not just express myself more openly than I could to any person; I create myself." Susan Sontag

5). Reduce stress and anxiety: It is possible to relieve your mind of negative thoughts by writing down your emotions. Moreover, during the writing process, you may discover a solution you had not previously considered.

"I never wrote things down to remember; I always wrote things down so I could forget."
Matthew McConaughey

6). Find inspiration: Journaling is a great time to brainstorm and run with your ideas. Free writing may even produce unexpected surprises in the form of ideas or solutions.

"I write for the same reason I breathe – because if I didn't, I would die." Isaac Asimov

7). Strengthen memory: By writing down your thoughts, you can reduce intrusive thoughts about negative events and increase your working memory. By simply taking notes, it is reported you are strengthening your brain.

"Journaling is paying attention to the inside for the purpose of living well from the inside out."
Lee Wise

By journaling, successful people know they can take stock of their day, set goals, track progress, gain self-confidence, improve writing skills, reduce stress and anxiety, find inspiration, and strengthen their memory. Now the question is, do you journal? If not, why?

MENTAL HEALTH/THERAPY

Successful people are well-educated on how important mental health is. They have learned to identify troubling situations, including paying attention to how they think and feel about them. They understand that it's important to pay attention to what they say to themselves (self-talk), and how they interpret what each situation means. They might be thinking negatively, or they might be thinking positively.

> **"If you are not happy with something, you should change it. So, I went to a lot of therapy, and finally, I am able to speak up for myself: You are going to hear me roar!"** Katy Perry

Successful people have learned to identify troubling conditions or situations that trigger emotional distress. They are aware of their thoughts and beliefs, especially negative thoughts, and negative self-talk. They have learned to challenge negative and inaccurate thinking patterns or statements, such as all-or-nothing thinking, jumping to negative conclusions, mistaking feelings for facts, distorting or filtering information, and reverting to negative self-talk.

"I believe that a different therapy must be constructed for each patient because each has a unique story." Irvin D. Yalom

Successful people know that therapy offers a broad scope of benefits that can help resolve conflict, relieve anxiety or stress, cope with major life changes, learn to manage unhealthy reactions, come to terms with an ongoing or serious physical health problem, recover from physical or sexual abuse, and to sleep better.

Many successful people including Ariana Grande, Brian Wilson, Brooke Shields, Catherine Zeta-Jones, Charlize Theron, Demi Lovato, Emma Stone, Gwyneth Paltrow, Halle Berry, Herschel Walker, Jim Carrey, J. K. Rowling, Jessica Alba, Jon Hamm, Justin Bieber, Katy Perry, Kerry Washington, Kid Cudi, Kristen Bell, Lady Gaga, Megan Thee Stallion, Michael B. Jordan, Michael Phelps, Mike Wallace, Miley Cyrus, Oprah, Pete Davidson, Selena Gomez, Shailene Woodley, Zendaya, and others have openly shared their support of therapy.

"I would say that I began with a very edgy, very driven personality and after a sufficient amount of therapy over many, many years, I managed to become rather relaxed and happy." John Cleese

Therapy can help people and even bolster creativity, productivity, and passion through recognizing how their past is affecting their current state of being. In addition to helping, you work with your therapist to set your own treatment goals, learn to navigate internal and external barriers, and enhance both your resilience and confidence. Overall, therapy can assist you in working toward all kinds of goals.

Successful people have learned that therapy assists them in breaking bad habits and helps them address and change unhealthy patterns. Unhealthy thinking patterns can affect anyone, even successful people. These patterns are addressed before people end up being confused, not feeling as they're good enough, or suffering from other negative feelings.

"We may define therapy as a search for value."
Abraham Maslow

The benefit of therapy is that it allows a person to broaden their awareness of life, to not get stuck on one way of expressing their feelings, to explore ways of expressing themselves in healthy ways they may have been hiding from themselves, and to improve their quality of life and well-being.

Successful people utilize therapy in order to live their best life and remain healthy, happy, and mentally fit. How fit is your mental health?

READING

The message that we learn from our parents and teachers is that reading is the path to fulfillment and success, and it is. Think of the smartest person you know, and odds are you see them reading for hours on end. Those who become successful are usually those who make it a habit to read voraciously.

> **"The more that you read, the more things you will know. The more that you learn, the more places you'll go."** Dr. Seuss

People who are successful don't just read anything. They are highly selective about what they consume, choosing to be educated over entertained. They believe that books provide the means by which we can gain knowledge and experience.

> **"I'm reading so much and exposing myself to so many new ideas. It almost feels like the chemistry and the structure of my brain is changing so rapidly sometimes."** Emma Watson

Most successful people prefer to read educational books and publications over novels, tabloids, and magazines.

They especially seek inspiration and guidance from biographies and autobiographies of other successful people.

> **"When I think about how I understand my role as a citizen, setting aside being president...the most important stuff I've learned I think I've learned from novels."** Barack Obama

Many successful people in the world read up to 50 books per year (Warren Buffett, Bill Gates, Elon Musk, Oprah, Reese Witherspoon, and many others).

> **"I wouldn't be a songwriter if it wasn't for books that I loved as a kid, and I think that when you can escape into a book, it trains your imagination to think big and to think that more can exist than what you see."** Taylor Swift

Here are four steps to building good reading habits and setting reading goals:

1). Set a goal to read 20 pages per day and make it a habit of reading each day.

2). Read with a purpose. Select books or articles that you actually will enjoy and want to learn about. Nobody wants to read just to read.

3). Remove distractions. Pick an environment where you can focus and unwind into a book. Place your phone on silent, shut off unneeded lights, and you will be able to focus on your book.

4). Do not read in bed. Bed is for sleeping, and your mind is triggered to think of your bed as a place of rest. If you read in bed, you're more likely to have difficulty focusing and possibly falling asleep.

"Books were my path to personal freedom, I learned to read at age 3 and soon discovered there was a whole world to conquer that went beyond our farm in Mississippi." Oprah

Remember, knowledge is power. It's a great way to learn new things, increase brain function, access information to help you become more successful, and it's a healthy habit. How many hours do you read each week? What will you read next?

TIME

Few would argue against the notion that time is the most precious commodity. It's a commodity we cannot purchase regardless of how much money we possess. No two people have the same amount of time available to them in their lives. Unfortunately, not everyone realizes that with each passing minute, hour, or day that time is gone forever. Successful people, on the other hand, are very aware of the value of their time.

> **"Your time is limited, so don't waste it living someone else's life.... Don't let the noise of others' opinions drown out your own inner voice. And most important, have the courage to follow your heart and intuition."** Steve Jobs

Successful people maximize their time by identifying what really matters. Successful people make sure that something is worthy of their time before they devote any energy to it. Goal setting is a priority with successful people. They make sure to chart out where they need to be on any given task and when they expect it to be complete. They do not go blindly into an activity.

"Don't be fooled by the calendar. There are only as many days in the year as you make use of. One man gets only a week's value out of a year while another man gets a full year's value out of a week." Charles Richards

Avoiding distractions is something successful people are good at. Have you ever had great intentions and then realized you just wasted time looking at a social media app, texting, or simply letting the day slip away? Successful people are different. They take essential time for breaks, family, and relaxation, but they maximize their work time to be the most proficient they can be.

How successful people maximize their time:

1). They delegate. Successful people know there's the right person for each job, and they do not get caught up taking on every aspect of an assignment or micro-manage their associates.

2). Breaking down goals into manageable tasks is essential. Successful people utilize SMART goals to meet deadlines and utilize their time effectively.

3). Prioritizing is a skill successful people have had to master in their careers. There's a time and a place for everything, and successful people prioritize what task needs to be tackled first.

4). Doing away with distractions, small-talk, busywork, and wasting time is fundamental for successful people. It comes down to what is more important - achieving a goal or temporarily enjoying a moment.

5). Maximizing time is a superpower of successful people. They will often exercise and listen to audio books, use commute time to make calls, and utilize every moment of their day to its fullest.

"He who every morning plans the transactions of that day and follows that plan carries a thread that will guide him through the labyrinth of the most-busy life." Victor Hugo

6). Having a structured plan is part of a successful person's repertoire. They make lists so that they will have time to meditate, eat, exercise, work, spend time with family, relax, and sleep.

7). Tackling one task at a time is the best route to take. Successful people know that multi-tasking has been proven to be highly ineffective and very inefficient. Successful people are highly focused on each task until it is complete.

8). Being passionate and highly motivated are a dynamic combination. When your goal is the thing that drives you, it's hard not to be successful. You cannot pay a person to be passionate, yet passion is a great motivator and a powerful attribute. Successful people are always the most passionate and motivated people in the room.

"Once you have mastered time, you will understand how true it is that most people overestimate what they can accomplish in a year - and underestimate what they can achieve in a decade!" Tony Robbins

Realizing time is your greatest commodity sets you apart from everyone else who may be mindlessly letting life slip away minute by minute. Successful people maximize their time and avoid distractions, and you should too. Today is the best day for you to evaluate how you spend your time. Are you maximizing your time?

ACCEPT FAILURE

Yes, you read that correctly, but successful people don't accept failure as a permanent state. They see it as part of the process until they succeed. Their success is the result of having a different mindset. Successful people constantly explore, experiment, and learn from mistakes. This is something that is rare among other people because they fear failure.

"If you're not prepared to be wrong, you'll never come up with anything original." Sir Ken Robinson

Successful people make it a habit to work from a mindset that accepts failure as part of the creative process. The most successful people understand that the worst form of failure is fear of not being able to achieve your goal which prevents you from attempting it at all. Therefore, the mindset of try until I succeed is the mantra of the successful person.

"I have not failed. I've just found 10,000 ways that won't work." Thomas A. Edison

Successful people do not see failure as being diametrically opposite of success. They see it as part of their education, learning, and growth. Successful people are not quitters by nature. They are people who walk to the beat of their own drum. They are able to see the positive in elements of each process they undertake.

> **"Winners are not afraid of losing. But losers are. Failure is part of the process of success. People who avoid failure also avoid success."**
> Robert T. Kiyosaki

Successful people are brave people. That's not to say brave people are never afraid because they are. The difference is they push through the fear because they believe the fear is worth the reward. Moreover, they understand that part of being brave is doing things that cause a person to be out of their comfort zone, things that are ambiguous, and stuff that is outright fear-inducing.

Lessons learned through failure:

1). Realize that all is not lost when things don't go as planned.

2). Redefine priorities and what's important.

3). Reshape values and what drives a person.

4). Being forced to revise an approach to solving a problem or creating a solution.

5). Mental and emotional resiliency is reinforced.

6). Realization that success isn't everything. The value can be found throughout the journey.

7). Re-evaluate one's methods and approach.

8). Reach out for expert advice or mentoring.

9). Manage time and budget better.

10). Anticipate and identify obstacles sooner.

11). Learn not to take no for an answer.

12). Reinvigorate passion and desire.

13). Identify habits that may have caused failure.

14). Failure is not an option and don't quit.

Successful people make it a habit to be in uncomfortable situations, so that in time, it does not induce the same amount of fear. In time, uncertainty can be exciting and make life more colorful. This is not to suggest successful people take unnecessary risks or are fiscally irresponsible. They simply are willing to take on projects that may result in temporary failure, but that are incredible learning opportunities. Do you fear failure, or is it part of your process?

CHASE YOUR OWN GOALS

The tenet of being your own boss is favored by successful people since it offers them the opportunity to pursue their own dreams instead of working to chase someone else's. Or more succinctly, successful people do not waste their time fulfilling the dreams of others. They have a vision. They devise their own objectives and work hard to fulfill them. They know if they spend all of their time living other people's dreams, then they will not reach their own potential in life.

"Believe you can and you're halfway there."
Theodore Roosevelt

Steps to chasing your own goals:

1). Search out your goal: Getting your dream off the ground requires asking questions. Talk to experts within your field. Don't feel embarrassed if you're less knowledgeable and powerful than them. Successful people realize that, in time, they too will become experts because they chose to seek out education and advice from experts.

"If you want to conquer fear, don't sit home and think about it. Go out and get busy."
Dale Carnegie

2). Be fearless: the more you commit to your goal the more likely you are to succeed. Take incremental advances toward your goal and before long you will be moving leaps and bounds. Successful people make taking risks a habit, and you should too. Eventually, you won't fear failure as you learn to take risks. You will learn to accept failure as a learning experience as you pursue your goals.

"The only thing worse than starting something and failing ... is not starting something."
Seth Godin

3). Have foresight and plan ahead: Successful people make it a habit to plan ahead. When you plan ahead, you will be able to identify the risks, prioritize them, and create a plan of attack. You can implement your plan without fear of failure once it's ready, and you'll see positive results. At times, you may still face failure. If you do, the best way to overcome this is to continue to plan well ahead so that you maintain your confidence as you try again.

"If you can dream it, you can do it." Walt Disney

4). Dream big and believe: Successful people know that the cumulative effect of planning, executing, building a foundation, and having the courage to pursue their dream make it impossible to not achieve far more than they expected. Add in that they dream big and back their dream with the belief they are prepared to succeed. Never underestimate the power of optimism and planning.

"Press on. Nothing in the world can take the place of persistence. Talent will not; nothing is more common than unsuccessful men with talent. Genius will not; the world is full of educated derelicts. Persistence and determination alone are omnipotent." Ray Kroc

How big is your dream, and how much do you believe in yourself?

VALUE SOLITUDE

Successful people know that time alone will provide them the possibility of working through their problems and allow them to increase their productivity. It is because solitude creates an atmosphere of contemplation and introspection where they can discover who they are and where they need to be.

"One of the greatest necessities in America is to discover creative solitude." Carl Sandburg

Everyone needs some affirmation of who they are and some connection with themselves. It is easy to lose our connection with ourselves as we are constantly distracted by friends, gadgets, and unnecessary demands. Successful people make it a habit to find solitude in order to reconnect with their inner self.

"I think there's a lot to be said for keeping your own counsel." Daniel Craig

Benefits of solitude:

1). Increases empathy: Spending time alone helps you develop more compassion for people who don't fit into your inner circle.

2). Increases productivity: People perform better in private. People who are surrounded by other people are less productive.

"My music is very personal. I've created it in solitude." Dwight Yoakam

3). Increases creativity: You can become more creative when you are able to be alone with your thoughts.

4). Mental Health: Research shows people who are able to tolerate solitude are happier, more satisfied in their lives, and are better at managing stress.

5). Benefits goal planning: Solitude can allow you to reflect on your goals, your progress, and what you want to change about yourself.

"I live in solitude. I have need of solitude to do the next day's work. I must have complete calm." Yves Saint Laurent

Successful people value solitude because it increases empathy, productivity, creativity, mental health, and goal planning. Besides, when you're alone, you can make your own decisions without outside interference, thus giving you a deeper understanding of who you are. How comfortable are you with solitude?

FEEDBACK

Positive or negative feedback can determine one's potential for success, but how one reacts to it will define it. Successful people believe they can improve their lives through constructive criticism, which they view as an opportunity to do better. They believe everyone could benefit from feedback and make it a habit to share it in a constructive manner.

> **"To acquire knowledge, one must study; but to acquire wisdom, one must observe."**
> Marilyn vos Savant

Successful people believe feedback allows for important decisions to be made based on valuable information and observation. Successful people are great at accepting feedback and know it has great benefits when shared productively.

> **"There is always space for improvement, no matter how long you've been in the business."**
> Oscar De La Hoya

Feedback factors:

1). Feedback is not static and is active through every aspect of our daily activity and interactions.

2). In order to feel appreciated and valued, the person providing the feedback will need to hear that their feedback has been heard and understood.

3). It's useful to provide feedback to people, as this helps them feel valued and helps in making decisions. Leaders know people appreciate being asked for their opinions and can be motivated to improve performance.

4). Feedback improves decision making and performance.

5). Continual feedback provides a conversation loop that improves learning and cohesion.

"I think it's very important to have a feedback loop, where you're constantly thinking about what you've done and how you could be doing it better." Elon Musk

Successful people know feedback is static, that it allows people to feel they are valued and understood, it allows for informed decision making, and it improves performance. How are you at giving and receiving feedback?

PERSEVERANCE

Perseverance is one of the keys to success. No one succeeds in life if they give up. Successful people never let their goals slip from their grasp, no matter how many times they've been knocked down. Successful people know people succeed when they don't give in to the temptation to quit.

> **"Pursue success, long after the sane person would have given up."** Heidi Klum

Rather than seeing challenges and setbacks as obstacles, we should embrace them as opportunities for growth and development. After a setback, it's time to re-evaluate, strategize, and take the next steps that can lead to success. Remember, it is the way we respond to failure that contributes most to our growth as successful individuals.

> **"A failure is not always a mistake. It may simply be the best one can do under the circumstances. The real mistake is to stop trying."** B.F. Skinner

Perseverance is often more important to success than talent or innate qualities. That does not mean talent does not matter, but it only goes so far without patience and persistence. We rarely reach our greatest achievements by simply being who we are. More often, it is through what we accomplish, and how we accomplish it.

>**"Through perseverance many people win success out of what seemed destined to be certain failure."** Benjamin Disraeli

At times, it can seem like nothing is going right and everyone else is accomplishing their goals. Remember, you're only competing against yourself. This is the time when you need to take a short break and regroup, refocus on your vision, meditate, journal, reflect on what went wrong, seek out counsel or mentorship, encourage yourself by remembering all the successes you've had throughout life, and then start anew with positivity.

>**"Failures are infinitely more instructive than successes."** George Clooney

If you're ever thinking about giving up, and you feel you simply cannot see progress, I want you to think about a parable I'm about to share regarding the Chinese Bamboo Tree. The phenomenal orator Les Brown delivered this parable in a church sermon. It's a lesson in the power of perseverance.

The Chinese Bamboo Tree, like any other plant, requires soil, water, and fertilizer, but it requires something more than these elements. It requires patience and perseverance. Chinese Bamboo Tree farmers must plant the seed, keep it watered and nutrient rich, cultivate the soil, and have a long-term commitment for it to grow.

After the first year of watering, adding nutrients and cultivating the soil every day, the Chinese Bamboo Tree shows no visual sign of progress. Not one sprout rises from the ground. Nevertheless, the farmer continues to nurture the seed.

After the second year of watering, adding nutrients and cultivating the soil, there are still no signs of growth. Again, not one sign the seed has sprouted. It is the same story for the third and fourth years as well. Despite 1,460 continual days of nurturing, the seed does not appear to have grown. Not a single sign of progress.

Over the years, people look at the Chinese Bamboo Tree farmer as though he is crazy. They ask, "Who would invest so much time into something that doesn't grow?" They doubt and ridicule him as they point out that nothing has grown on his patch of soil. Still, the Chinese Bamboo Tree farmer perseveres, nurturing the seed as he has done for the past four years.

Then, in the fifth year, something miraculous happens. Something that leaves everyone except the Chinese Bamboo Tree farmer in awe. The Chinese Bamboo Tree sprouts and grows 90 feet in just five weeks (Yes, it really does grow to such heights in a five-week span).

The question then is raised, did the seed sit dormant for five years and then grow rapidly, or did it grow for five years unseen? The answer is it grew for five years. In order for the tree to be able to support its stellar growth, it spent five years growing a strong and vast root network. Below the surface, it was preparing for the day it would rise to tower 90 feet in the sky.

Like trees, we cannot always see our growth and progress. Cast aside your doubters. Stay your course. Think of the Chinese Bamboo Tree when you're struggling, and no one believes in you.

Think of the Chinese Bamboo Tree when you desire immediate results for something that realistically needs time to grow. Remember, you are setting your roots strong and deep in order for you to reach the highest levels of success.

Often growth is slow and painful, long, and difficult, and at times frustrating and debilitating, but if you continue to nurture your goals, you will persevere like the Chinese Bamboo Tree. Are you prepared to persevere?

POSITIVE ATTITUDE

We are naturally negatively biased. Negativity bias is a useful evolutionary trait as it keeps the brain fully aware of threats and dangers in our environment. For millennia, this was crucial for survival. While focused on our surroundings, our brains were constantly monitoring for danger. Therefore, we inherently have a negative bias about the world based solely on survival mechanisms.

> **"Once you replace negative thoughts with positive ones, you'll start having positive results."** Willie Nelson

We have been suffering for centuries from the unfortunate result of our brain's evolution not keeping pace with the safety advances our civilized society has given us. As a result, our brains have retained this inherent trait. If you maintain this primitive negative outlook, it is almost impossible to be successful in our world today.

> **"In order to carry a positive action, we must develop here a positive vision."** Dalai Lama

A positive attitude can change everything and counteract negative bias. According to successful individuals, positive attitude is the main reason for their success because it gives them the strength to overcome difficult circumstances. Positive attitude not only helps you to increase your confidence, but it also helps you accomplish your goals successfully.

"Positive thinking will let you do everything better than negative thinking will." Zig Ziglar

Reasons to fight being negative:

1). Having a negative attitude suppresses the prefrontal cortex, which is important to creativity, decision-making, impulse control, memory, and seeing solutions as opposed to problems.

2). Negative thinking results in chronic stress, which can result in inflammation throughout the body that can lead to disease. Health problems will increase difficulty to concentrate on success.

3). The negative traits you possess can make you toxic. Others who are positive and like to surround themselves with positivity will avoid associating with you.

"Positive thinking is more than just a tagline. It changes the way we behave. And I firmly believe that when I am positive, it not only makes me better, but it also makes those around me better." Harvey Mackay

Reasons to be positive include:

1). Positive people have more energy, excitement, and self-confidence, so they can set higher goals and exert more effort to achieve their goals. The positive person is also more resilient, which means they can bounce back after setbacks and persevere.

2). Positivity broadens our focus where negativity narrows it. By broadening one's focus, it is easier to see solutions and make healthier and more creative decisions.

3). Those who are positive tend to be more connected to others and experience healthy emotions. The more connected a person is - the more likely they are to experience personal and social growth. It's easier to accomplish goals when a person feels a sense of emotional support.

4). Positive people experience better physical health. Positivity promotes better health, less stress, and an increased immune system, which allows them to focus on enjoying their life and focusing on success.

"I've always followed my heart and pursued my dreams, and I imagine that people find that inspiring. I definitely want to project a positive energy out into the world." Britney Spears

Successful people make a conscious choice to remain positive even in the face of despair. They understand that they are naturally wired for negative bias and therefore take a proactive approach to maintaining positivity. They welcome positivity and the benefit of more energy, self-confidence, connectedness, better emotional and physical health, and the ability to enjoy life. How positive are you in the face of challenges?

TAKE RISKS

When you are afraid to try out new things in life, you cannot achieve anything extraordinary in your life. It is imperative to take calculated risks if you hope to achieve great things in life. Successful people are risk-takers who never hesitate to take risks. They know that it provides them with a variety of opportunities that make their lives more fulfilling.

> **"Only those who will risk going too far can possibly find out how far it is possible to go."**
> T.S. Eliot

Taking risks allows us to expand our chances at new opportunities. By broadening opportunities, we increase the variables and effectively increase the possibility of success. In other words, we are more likely to have good luck (opportunity presents itself) by putting ourselves out there and taking educated risks rather than if we sit things out and wait for a safer opportunity.

> **"Anything that is successful is a series of mistakes."** Billie Joe Armstrong

Successful people learn from taking risks. When we take risks, we can learn from both our successes and failures.

Sometimes, in a matter of hours, our knowledge changes exponentially. From taking risks, we have insight that we would never have achieved by playing it safe and waiting on the sidelines of life.

> **"You'll always miss 100% of the shots you don't take."** Wayne Gretzky

Successful people are not following a careless call to risk everything, but they are heeding the call to step out of their comfort zone. If they fail, it is simply a learning experience that will only strengthen their knowledge and resolve. In short, failing is the key to success because it allows us to redefine success and make learning a centerpiece of personal development and experience.

> **"Trust your own instinct. Your mistakes might as well be your own, instead of someone else's."**
> Billy Wilder

Is the fear of taking risks holding you back? What are you willing to try regardless of the anticipated results? How far are you willing to go? How much are you willing to risk in order to be successful?

ATTENTION TO DETAIL

The devil is in the details. Paying attention to details means being thorough and accurate when handling tasks. It means being able to focus on what matters and being efficient and effective while carrying out your duties. Attention to detail means continuously allocating cognitive resources effectively to accomplish tasks.

"The success of a production depends on the attention paid to detail." David O. Selznick

Many people neglect details, which costs them time and money. Paying attention to details can improve things in terms of accuracy, time, and quality. It is a desirable quality for successful people because they don't want to repeat a single task again and again, wasting their valuable time and resources.

"It's the little things that make the big things possible. Only close attention to the fine details of any operation makes the operation first class." J. Willard Marriott

Five primary skills that will help with attention to detail:

1). Active listening refers to listening in such a way that keeps you engaged with your conversation partner in a positive way. It is listening attentively while others speak, paraphrasing, and reflecting without giving judgment or advice. Active listening should include maintaining eye contact, using body language, paraphrasing, and listening before offering a genuine response.

2). Organizational skills include the ability to manage your time and resources expertly. Although organizational skills can vary based on your career, they usually involve creating an orderly workspace, meeting deadlines, paying attention to details, and communicating effectively.

3). Analytical skills include critical thinking, data analysis, research, and communication. Analytical skills are skills that help a person identify and solve complex problems. This skill allows a person to break information into smaller categories in order to be able to infer conclusions.

"It's the little details that are vital. Little things make big things happen." John Wooden

4). Time management skills include prioritizing work, working within timelines, setting up goals, scheduling, focusing on specific tasks rather than multi-tasking, and maintaining motivation to complete assignments.

5). Observation skills are the ability to use your senses to recognize, analyze, and recall your surroundings. It involves being present and aware of details.

Active listening, organizational skills, analytical skills, time management skills, and observation skills are all part of being attentive to details. In addition to attention to detail, you will also be able to see more specifically what the big picture looks like when you hone these skills. Are you focused on the details?

BALANCED LIFE

Those who are successful know that taking time off from their busy lives can give them more energy and power. Therefore, they keep a healthy balance between work and life. Successful people understand with their hectic schedules that it is important to maintain a well-balanced life for their health and well-being, to improve their mood, to reduce their stress, and to be able to continue to succeed.

> **"Everything in life... has to have balance."**
> Donna Karan

Successful people know balance is achieved over time, not over the course of a single day. They aim for a realistic schedule, not a perfect one. Some days may be focused on work; others might be dedicated to leisure activities or spending time with family.

> **"The hardest thing to find in life is balance -
> especially the more success you have."**
> Celine Dion

Make it a habit to find a career that you love. By doing so, it makes balance much easier and less draining. Let's face it, if you hate what you're doing, and it is toxic, sooner or later, it's going to destroy you. Successful people leave toxic careers behind and pursue things they love.

> **"Balance is good, because one extreme or the other leads to misery, and I've spent a lot of my life at one of those extremes."** Trent Reznor

Your overall physical, emotional, and psychological health should be your priority. To maintain balance, take time to recharge, unplug from work and devices, read a book, exercise, meditate, get a massage, go to therapy, pursue your hobbies, find something you desire to start as an activity, or spend time with friends and family. Decompressing is essential for longevity and helps maintain or lead to even greater success.

> **"I think what's really important is finding a balance of mind, body and spirit."** Jennifer Lopez

It's important to take time off for a vacation and switch off from work completely. No matter how long the vacation lasts, it's important to recharge both physically and mentally. In addition to helping a person recharge, vacations can inspire, positively change, and reinvigorate a person.

> **"We've just learned how to balance ourselves a little better so that we're happier way more of the time than not, and, you know, being happy**

is a radical and desirable act if you ask me."
Anthony Kiedis

Making time is important to successful people, and it should be important to you too. Family and friends are one of your greatest commodities. You should make sure you spend quality time with them for your benefit and for theirs.

> **"I've always tried to balance my life with what is good for me but also keeping in mind how it affects somebody else."** Roger Staubach

Setting boundaries is a necessity, not only to keep people at work from contacting you at all hours, but so that you also maintain personal boundaries. It is imperative to set boundaries and goals - and stick to them.

> **"The trick to balance is to not make sacrificing important things become the norm."** Simon Sinek

Certainly, there are long hours and sacrifices made by successful people but having a balanced life will afford you more success, a better personal and family life, and reward you with better health and longevity. How is your work/life balance? Are you living a balanced life?

TRUST YOUR GUT

Have you ever met with someone, and you immediately knew you could not work with them? Maybe you were sitting in an interview. Within moments you knew in your gut that you were not going to enjoy working with this person, only to come to that certainty at the end of your meeting. This is your intuition at work.

> **"The more you trust your intuition, the more empowered you become, the stronger you become, and the happier you become."**
> Gisele Bündchen

Hundreds of thousands of years ago, instinct and intuition kept human survival alive. As we've evolved, we've learned to rely on a treasure trove of data and education in making decisions, which has often consigned intuition as ineffective, but it shouldn't be relegated to the past. Intuition is a cognitive process that engages your gut to put you on alert and keep you safe.

> **"Statistics rarely drive me. Feelings, intuition, and gut instinct do."** Jason Fried

Gut-brain connections make it possible for emotional experiences to manifest based on sensory data to be signaled as gastrointestinal distress. When you experience anxiety, fear, or you're certain something is wrong, you might experience stomach pain or nausea. This is your gut telling you to take notice and be alert. Gut instinct isn't based solely on the present. Gut instinct is connected to the unconscious. It makes predictions and generates responses based on past experiences.

> **"Mathematical reasoning may be regarded rather schematically as the exercise of a combination of two facilities, which we may call intuition and ingenuity."** Alan Turing

It is important to not confuse gut instinct with anxiety as they both can generate similar response. Gut instinct is different in that it only triggers a response in very specific engagements and leads to concrete decision making. It is not based on worrying which is common with anxiety. Anxiety tends to linger, where gut reaction is in the here and now, and then it's gone upon the end of the interaction.

> **"I believe I am a brilliant and gifted guide, that I have been given a tremendous intuition."**
> Mel Robbins

Successful people have learned that success comes from making the right decision in the right situation, and sometimes following our gut is the best course of action.

You still need to make a decision that is based on facts, including data and logic. You must rule out bias before ruling on the side of intuition. Successful people trust their gut, but they will follow up with further investigation before passing on a partnership or a business venture.

> **"Intuition is the key to everything, in painting, filmmaking, business - everything. I think you could have an intellectual ability, but if you can sharpen your intuition, which they say is emotion and intellect joining together, then a knowingness occurs."** David Lynch

Intuition is another tool that we should not disregard in our choice of business partners and encounters in general. If something doesn't feel right, trust your gut. How well do you trust your intuition?

KNOW YOUR ROLE

It's no secret that successful people tend to be perfectionists and strive to be the best at everything they do, but they don't invest time in other operations that don't serve their overall goal. Successful people stay in their lane. They know who they are and what they do best. Successful people focus on their chosen role and stick with the goal at hand without micromanaging or monologuing their team.

> **"When everything is coming your way, you're probably in the wrong lane."** Tom Snyder

Because it's not always easy to recognize your strengths and weaknesses, people often try to take on too much. Before a person finds themselves in a crucial decision that needs to be made, it's best to take inventory of what you're great at and what your focus area should not include.

> **"When you're in your own lane, there's no traffic."** Ava DuVernay

It's not hard to acknowledge Don Shula as one of the greatest football coaches to ever live, but we certainly wouldn't have wanted him to suit up for the Superbowl. Mr. Shula's role was coaching, not playing. He is best leading from the sidelines, not the field. There is a role for everyone, and successful people don't micromanage. They utilize their assets effectively, serve their role, and allow others to serve theirs.

"You have to surround yourself with good people and help them to do what they do well, as opposed to micromanaging." Robbie Myers

Why should people know their role and stay in their lanes? For numerous reasons, including everyone has a role - and if not, then they're not needed. Successful people are usually successful because they are surrounded by talented individuals - each with more expertise than others in their specific area. Successful people make it a habit to utilize the talent around them. They allow people to speak on what they know and not try to be the expert on everything themselves. Successful people realize that as a team, we are more valuable than the sum of our parts.

"A leader's job is to lead and protect. That's their job, and it's the people within the organization - their job is to get the work done."
Simon Sinek

We can accomplish more if we focus on our area of expertise. This is not to say a singer/songwriter/producer can't take on all three roles. The three roles are still in their lane, but where they may not want to expand to is being their own booking agent or marketing person. Most often, a lot more can be accomplished in less time by each person staying in their lane and focusing on a specific role.

> **"Don't believe the hype. I don't care how many number ones you have at the box office; I don't care how much they say you're great, don't believe it. Just stay in your lane and do what you're supposed to do."** Tyler Perry

Successful people wear many hats, and they have an extensive skill set, but they don't lead by swerving across lanes, and neither should you. Successful people know their role, and so should you. Have you ever taken on a role that would have been better served by another more experienced team member? What role serves you and your projects best?

ROOT CAUSE

When things go wrong, and sooner or later things do, successful people want to get to the root of the problem. By identifying and understanding the root cause of a problem, successful people know it can be fixed and avoided in the future. A root cause analysis begins by identifying what actually went wrong. It asks what problem do you hope to resolve?

Here are the five steps to identifying root cause:

1). Realize the problem. There are three basic types of problems:

A). Material-based problems: Material problems happen when a part of a material item malfunctions in some way, such as when a piece of machinery breaks down.

B). People-based problems: Whenever an issue is caused by human error, it is deemed a people-based problem.

C). Organizational-based problems: They are problems within an organization that are caused by company processes or policies.

It is important for you to understand that what may appear on the surface to be solely a people-based problem may in fact be a material-based or organizational problem or vice-versa.

For example, it may seem that a there is a material-based problem because a machine is no longer operational. Further investigation may suggest it's a people-based problem because the roof over the machine was not maintained. But if it turns out company policy did not allow repair of the roof; it is then an organizational-based problem at the root.

"We cannot solve our problems with the same level of thinking that created them."
Albert Einstein

2). Collect information: As you work to identify a problem's root cause, it is helpful to get a multitude of perspectives. Ask your employees, who deal with this problem area on a daily basis, for their input. Their insight will prove valuable.

"Erroneous assumptions can be disastrous."
Peter Drucker

3). Identify causal factors: Find out if there are any other problems coexisting with the current one that you're facing. Setting up a timeline and asking these kinds of questions will allow you to identify the cause of your problem.

"But to measure cause and effect...you must ensure that a simple correlation, however tempting it may be, is not mistaken for a cause."
Neil deGrasse Tyson

4). Draw conclusions: You have identified the problem and its symptoms at this point in the root cause analysis process. You have also gathered sufficient data, relying on the knowledge and experience of your employees to do so, and have narrowed down to determine each causal factor.

5). Implement changes: After identifying the root cause/s for the problem at hand, collecting information, identifying causal factors, and drawing conclusions, you should have to develop and implement a practical solution to prevent it from happening again in the future. Can you utilize root cause analysis for any of your current problems?

"Each problem that I solved became a rule, which served afterwards to solve other problems." René Descartes

Root cause analysis allows a person to realize the problem and all related factors, and then implement changes. It acknowledges what actually went wrong as opposed to what might have gone wrong. Finding the root cause is the best way to solve problems and avoid them being repeated in the future. Have you ever performed a root cause analysis?

NOT AFRAID TO SUCCEED

Successful people are not afraid to succeed. They're willing to do what it takes, including receiving extra attention, risking envy from their peers, having future bars set higher, and realizing that success may change them. Often, people self-sabotage because they're afraid that if they succeed, then they will be expected to succeed all the time. Successful people are willing to accept the additional expectations and truly believe that they are worthy of being where they are at in their career.

"Don't let the fear of striking out hold you back." Babe Ruth

People who are not afraid to succeed make it a habit to set high goals. They do not procrastinate, but rather attack their work vigorously. They are often called perfectionists, but they do not use perfectionism as an excuse to quit if things are not going perfect. And they are conscious that they need to avoid being self-destructive, or they could lose everything.

You cannot reach a high level of success if you feel guilty about asserting yourself into a key role or into competition for success. Successful people work diligently to remain calm and not get anxious or cause long-term anxiety over surpassing co-workers or others in their industry. They are not fearful of the pressure that comes with having to perform at their best.

"Fear defeats more people than any other one thing in the world." Ralph Waldo Emerson

Even successful people have their doubts at times, and sometimes have to overcome imposter syndrome. What is imposter syndrome? People who have imposter syndrome feel they're a fraud and doubt their abilities. This condition mostly affects high-achieving people, who have difficulty accepting their achievements.

"Fear is the enemy of logic." Frank Sinatra

Many suffering from fear of success question if they're worthy of recognition. Successful people overcome their fears and imposter syndrome by visualizing success, eating well, maintaining exercise and their health, socializing with friends and family, meditating, journaling, and being mindful. Do you feel you are deserving of success?

HEALTHY INTERNAL DIALOGUE

Internal dialogue is the internal conversation our ego has with itself. It is the subconscious tone to which we apply logic, reasoning, and beliefs to situations, people, and events. It shapes the way we experience the world and shapes the way we perceive it. It is important to continually evaluate our internal dialogue.

> **"Cogito, ergo sum (I think, therefore I am)."**
> René Descartes

Successful people know too well that their internal dialogue has a significant impact on their perception of the world around them. If their internal dialogue is negative, it makes them see the world in negative terms. Comparatively, if their internal dialogue is positive, it makes them see the world in a positive light.

> **"Compare yourself to who you were yesterday, not to who someone else is today."**
> Jordan Peterson

For example, imagine a person calling us a loser has a value of one (one voice). If we internalize that message and accept it as a truth, our mind expands it, and the message will eventually become thousands of negative loops (thousands of voices). If we accept this as truth, our internal dialogue continues to compound this message until we wholeheartedly believe it to our core.

> **"Stop letting people who do so little for you control so much of your mind, feelings and emotions."** Will Smith

Here are six steps to help with generating positive internal dialogue:

1). Meditation: In order to master our internal dialogue, it helps to meditate daily. We have on average tens of thousands of thoughts each day, so calming our turbulent mind with positivity and silence is extremely beneficial.

2). Gratitude: As we choose to put our attention on those things, we can be grateful for, we move away from a negative mindset. Focusing on what's positive and uplifting in your life also trains you to be willing to seek out those kinds of experiences again and again.

3). Avoid negativity: It's hard to deny that negativity pervades our modern world. No matter where we turn, we can't escape it. Our brains, in part, are affected by negativity bias, which makes us more likely to notice negative circumstances and events than positive ones.

Consequently, we must do everything we can to stay away from negativity as often as possible.

4). Positive affirmations: Use affirmations (positive self-talk statements) to challenge self-sabotaging thoughts and defeat negative thoughts can help you begin to achieve your goals. By repeating affirmations frequently and believing them, you can achieve positive results.

5). Speech and behavior: When you consciously choose to practice impeccable speech and behavior, your internal dialogue automatically becomes positive. Similar to how your actions and speech reinforce your internal dialogue, you will automatically have a positive internal dialogue when you choose impeccable speech and behavior.

6). True nature: We need to take quiet breaks from our ego and the clutter of the world. When we identify with our true self, we instantly recognize that we are free from limitations and in a state of complete fulfillment.

"When you have experienced the depth of your inner self, the idea of enlightenment is no longer a goal to strive towards, but rather an attitude to maintain." Gary Hopkins

Successful people realize negative self-talk must not be internalized, and if it is, then it should not be accepted as truth. They know that there are steps such as meditation, gratitude, avoiding negativity, positive affirmations, speech and behavior, and remembering their true nature that can help them reinforce positive internal dialogue. How is your internal dialogue?

STRONG COMMUNICATOR

A person's ability to communicate effectively is seen as one of the most important traits by successful people. It all comes down to the ability to convey one's thoughts and ideas to others. People who are successful are able to effectively negotiate and convey pertinent information in their spoken and written communications.

> **"Words are, of course, the most powerful drug used by mankind."** Rudyard Kipling

Strong communication begins with listening. Successful people demonstrate their ability to listen attentively and engage others. You have to be able to gather information and understand what is being said, and then effectively respond and ensure your message is understood. Additionally, you must be able to pick up on non-verbal cues, as 70-90% of communication is reported to be non-verbal.

> **"When people talk, listen completely. Most people never listen."** Ernest Hemingway

A person who is highly successful can communicate effectively with a wide range of people and audiences, which is crucial to collaborating with them and sharing ideas. They are also able to gather feedback from them and understand what they need.

> **"The best speakers in the world are the best storytellers. They have a gift to not only tell a great story, but also share a lot of the details that many others wouldn't."** Larry Hagner

Think of Steve Jobs launching a new product, Martin Luther King, Jr. sharing "I Have a Dream," Warren Buffett addressing his shareholders, or John F. Kennedy expressing why we're going to the Moon. They are all strong communicators whose messages were loud and clear. There is not an ounce of ambiguity to what they're saying and what they are asking their audience to do.

Strong communication requires:

1). Active listening: Being engaged with your audience and not letting your internal dialogue distract from what they are expressing.

2). Interpreting non-verbal cues: Paying close attention to body language, facial expressions, and projecting positive body language shows you are engaged.

3). Manage expectations: Communicate clearly what is promised and what you will be delivering.

4). Conflict management: Maintain your integrity while accepting necessary changes, pushing back against non-productive ideas, and finding resolution.

5). Being concise: Stick to your main points and what the communication was intended to convey. Use language without ambiguity.

6). Value and differentiation: Clearly state what value you offer and what makes you different than all the rest.

7). Know your why: Understand the difference between what you do and why you do it. As Simon Sinek said, "People don't buy what you do; they buy why you do it. And what you do simply proves what you believe."

8). Call to action: Make it clear what you are asking the audience to do. Are they to make a purchase, vote, or simply feel better about an issue and leave inspired?

"Communication is a skill that you can learn. It's like riding a bicycle or typing. If you're willing to work at it, you can rapidly improve the quality of every part of your life." Brian Tracy

Strong communicators actively listen, interpret non-verbal cues, underpromise and overproduce, resolve conflict, speak concisely with authority and mastery of their subject, express value and differentiation, know their why, and have a call to action. Are you a strong and effective communicator? If not, what needs to change?

GROWTH MINDSET

People who are successful believe they can accomplish great things and are willing to work hard to do so. By cultivating a growth mindset, successful people encourage the belief that your basic qualities and traits can be improved and developed through effort and discipline.

> **"The strongest principle of growth lies in the human choice."** George Eliot

What exactly is a growth mindset? A growth mindset is the approach to facing challenges and overcoming setbacks. This mindset says that even if you struggle with certain skills, they aren't set in stone and that they can improve with time. Rather than viewing their flaws as permanent obstacles, they pursue self-improvement and accept challenges as opportunities.

> **"The people who are crazy enough to think they can change the world are the ones who do."**
> Steve Jobs

People who adopt this mindset are better able to manage turbulent times. A growth mindset sees failure as an opportunity for growth, as opposed to a fixed mindset that avoids challenges, gives up easily, and feels threatened by others' success.

> **"Between stimulus and response there is a space. In that space is our power to choose our response. In our response lies our growth and our freedom."** Viktor E. Frankl

Growth mindset includes:

1). Welcoming challenges: How can a person expect to grow without challenging themselves? Successful people accept challenges enthusiastically.

2). Mentorship: Essentially, mentoring is the process of transferring valuable knowledge, skills, and experience from a senior business leader.

3). Failure is learning: While failing can momentarily damage a person's self-esteem and confidence, in terms of a person's overall learning journey, failing provides a valuable lesson for people and an opportunity for growth.

4). Journaling: A great way to monitor successes and failures is to journal or take note of them to later be reviewed, show growth, and build confidence in a person's journey to success.

5). Surround yourself with talented people: Growth-minded people surround themselves with like-minded and talented individuals who can contribute to their professional and personal growth.

6). Disconnect/decompress: People with a growth mindset acknowledge they cannot be "on" at all times. They take time to disconnect and decompress from work.

7). Daily routines: In order to have a growth mindset it is important to document and develop daily habits to stay organized, motivated, and focused on the most important tasks.

8). Set goals: To help achieve growth, successful people set SMART goals in order to achieve specific, measurable, achievable, relevant, and timely goals.

9). Gut instinct: We have survived for millennia due to listening to our gut instinct. Whether it was surviving predators or a board meeting, successful people trust their gut.

10). Avoid stagnation: You cannot grow if you remain dormant. Though daily routines are great, they need to include new growth areas for learning and evolving.

"Nothing is impossible. The word itself says I'M POSSIBLE!" Audrey Hepburn

Successful people welcome challenges and are open to mentorship. They think of failure as an opportunity to learn, journal successes and failures to monitor growth, surround themselves with like-minded and talented individuals. They take time to decompress and disconnect from work, develop daily habits to be more productive, set SMART goals, listen to their gut and intuition, and avoid dormancy. Do you have a growth mindset?

PASSION

The world's most successful people are passionate about their dreams and goals, and they dedicate themselves feverishly to working towards them. Those who achieve success understand that passion will eventually lead to growth, and that growth will eventually lead to success.

There's no way to fake passion. It must emerge authentically from within. That's the reason you won't succeed at something you dislike. It must be something you are passionate about and to which you are willing to dedicate your time and effort.

> **"It is obvious that we can no more explain a passion to a person who has never experienced it than we can explain light to the blind."**
> T. S. Eliot

Only those individuals who are deeply committed to reaching their goals will actually succeed. That mindset will help shape their lives and circumstances in support of those ambitions.

> **"If you live without passion, you can go through life without leaving any footprints."** Betty White

Have you worked a job where every time you looked at the clock, it was as if time stood still? What a miserable experience. Contrarily, have you ever gotten blissfully lost in your work, and you suddenly realize the sun is going down? You're not sure where the day went. That's passion! Successful people live their passion. Remember, what drives you - also nourishes you.

Steve Jobs' Stanford commencement speech exudes passion:

> **"Your work is going to fill a large part of your life, and the only way to be truly satisfied is to do what you believe is great work. And the only way to do great work is to love what you do. If you haven't found it yet, keep looking. Don't settle. As with all matters of the heart, you'll know when you find it. And, like any great relationship, it just gets better and better as the years roll on. So, keep looking until you find it. Don't settle."** Steve Jobs

Successful people have long known passion fuels motivation and focus, opens creativity, fulfills a deep desire for happiness, attracts like-minded and passionate people, relieves stress, enhances positive attitudes, and nourishes the soul. What is your passion?

GOAL ORIENTED

The most successful people in the world have enormous dreams. They set goals to accomplish their dreams and become successful. They write down their goals and work on them consistently. Setting goals is one of the simplest habits to form if you want to be successful. The ability to set goals and achieve them is an empowering personal quality, as well as a trait that will greatly benefit you in your life.

> **"I have always lived my life by making lists. These vary from lists of people to call, lists of ideas, lists of companies to set up, lists of people who can make things happen. I also have lists of topics to blog about, lists of tweets to send, and lists of upcoming plans."**
> Sir Richard Branson

People who achieve success recognize the importance of being able to easily adapt to changes in circumstances. They periodically reassess their objectives to ensure they are on track. As a result, they evaluate their progress and make sure their goals remain relevant over time. If necessary, they adjust their goals or start over with newly formulated goals.

Goal-oriented people make it a habit to continually learn new things. Goal-oriented people are excellent at prioritizing clear and precise goals on what they need to do. They concentrate with a narrow focus on the most valuable use of their time. They are goal driven but work meticulously at one task at a time.

> **"You are never too old to set another goal or to dream a new dream."** C.S. Lewis

When you are goal oriented, you're focused on reaching or completing specific tasks to accomplish a particular outcome. Goal-oriented individuals are driven and motivated by a single purpose - accomplishing their goal. An individual who is goal-oriented stays motivated by setting targets via specific tasks. They accomplish each task toward their goal, but their work is motivated by the outcome.

Goal-oriented people start with the end in mind. They understand the significance of the decisions they are making and how they will affect the trajectory of their life. So much so, that they can imagine how this will be looked upon at the end of their life. What do your end results look like?

AMBITION

Successful people are usually the most ambitious people in a room. They pursue their goals without hesitation and go to great lengths to do it. In order to echo the mindset of successful people, you need to be extremely driven and as ambitious as them in order to do what it takes to fulfill your dreams. You have to be prepared to put in double the effort than everyone else. Remember, it's your dream.

> **"A man's worth is no greater than his ambitions."** Marcus Aurelius

Ambitious people set goals and stick to them. They set both short-term and long-term goals - and utilize daily task lists. Successful people take risks and are experts at turning unexpected results into gold. Think of the 3M Post-it note. Ambitious people are open to new ways of thinking. They are open to input from a variety of sources.

> **"Intelligence without ambition is a bird without wings."** Salvador Dalí

Without execution, goals are useless. Ambitious people are focused on execution and do not wait for the "perfect" time to take action. They are in a race against themselves, and they measure their successes and failures based on their goals - not external sources.

"Don't be afraid to be ambitious about your goals. Hard work never stops. Neither should your dreams." Dwayne Johnson

Ambitious people don't want to emulate others. They are determined to succeed on their own terms. Though they are known to be highly emotional, they also are able to temper excessive aggressive tendencies. This is offset by their internal drive, and it's that which makes them an inspiration to others.

"Ambition is enthusiasm with a purpose."
Frank Tyger

Ambitious people stick to their timelines. Remember, anyone can say they're going to change the world, but ambitious people will tell you how and when it will happen. Last, they surround themselves with other ambitious people who are willing to follow their vision to achieve a common goal. How ambitious are you?

OPTIMISM

Success comes from keeping yourself focused on the positive. While driving toward it, you maintain an objective and realistic perspective of the situation, sprinkled with a large helping of hopefulness and confidence. Successful people combine a positive outlook with an unbiased perspective when it comes to their present and future outlook. Optimists view struggle as opportunity - not as a negative situation.

> **"Optimism is a strategy for making a better future. Because unless you believe that the future can be better, you are unlikely to step up and take responsibility for making it so."**
> Noam Chomsky

Optimists do not fool themselves into believing that they will succeed easily. There's a difference between "I'm going to create this incredible thing," and "I'm going to create this incredible thing overnight." Though if anyone could attack such a project, it would be the optimist. Their optimism helps them remain nimble and flexible, seeking out new opportunities despite unfamiliar territory and risk.

> **"I believe any success in life is made by going into an area with a blind, furious optimism."**
> Sylvester Stallone

Additionally, they are honest with themselves and can admit mistakes. Optimists are not delusional, and just like other successful people, they do not blame others for their shortcomings. Though they may fall short at times, they have an overall positive attitude. They don't let negativity or pessimism encroach on their lives. Those distractions would make it nearly impossible for them to persevere through difficult circumstances.

> **"I am an optimist... I choose to be. There is a lot of darkness in our world, there is a lot of pain and you can choose to see that, or you can choose to see the joy. If you try to respond positively to the world, you will spend your time better."** Tom Hiddleston

Their approach to overcoming obstacles is realistic and practical, and they are persistent when it comes to working hard to achieve their goals. The more optimistic a person is, the more likely they are to invest, act, and put effort into achieving their goals. Optimistic people continually look forward to their goals.

Practice these approaches to become more optimistic:

1). Mindfulness: Being mindful is the ability to be fully present, aware of where we are, and what we are doing, and to not overreact or be overwhelmed by what takes place around us.

2). Gratitude: An expression of gratitude is an appreciation of what one has, and it is an acknowledgement of value that does not depend on money.

3). Journaling positive emotions: Writing down your positive thoughts and emotions is reported to improve optimism.

4). Cognitive restructuring: Replacing stress-inducing thoughts (cognitive distortions) with balanced thoughts that do not induce stress or negativity. This includes identifying automatic thoughts (negative thoughts), identifying cognitive distortions (all-or-nothing, black-and-white thinking), and disputing distortions (questioning if something is accurate, misrepresented, or overestimated?).

"Optimism is essential to achievement and it is also the foundation of courage and true progress." Nicholas M. Butler

When I arrived in Hollywood, and I was attending my first industry event, I had to remind myself to be fully present and focused in the here and now. Be aware of where I'm at (in Hollywood, where I belong), what I'm doing (pitching my talent agency), and not be overwhelmed by the room full of award-winning talent and industry veterans.

I focused on expressing my gratitude for this amazing opportunity no matter what the outcome, for I knew even missteps would be valuable lessons. And that regardless of successfully pitching my talent agency, my value isn't solely dependent on selling the business - but living this experience and promoting my clients.

Before entering the lion's den, I had to constantly remind myself that I deserved to be there, and that nobody was going to stand up and point me out as not belonging. I had to replace the cognitive distortions with healthy and productive thoughts, such as "I deserve to be here, or they wouldn't have invited me." I had to do away with the idea that the event would either be a success or failure (concrete thinking) - of which neither was true.

Successful people are focused, positive, objective, and they see struggle as opportunity. They are flexible, hopeful, honest, persistent, and hardworking. They are invested leaders, who own their mistakes and keep negativity at bay via mindfulness, gratitude, journaling, and cognitive restructuring. Are you optimistic? Have you ever had to challenge cognitive distortions?

CONFIDENCE

Confidence is a vital part of a positive attitude. Not only does it help you perform better, but it also helps you feel more relaxed when people are counting on you. Having confidence doesn't mean a person never has doubts. They just don't let those doubts internalize into fear. Successful people are not afraid of ambiguity or the unknown. They find challenges to be stimulating and the spice of life.

> **"Believe in yourself! Have faith in your abilities! Without a humble but reasonable confidence in your own powers you cannot be successful or happy."** Norman Vincent Peale

In order to be truly successful, one should learn to harness these concerns and put aside their fears. You should be fearless in taking action and going after your dreams. You should have the courage and self-confidence to test out innovative ideas by crushing doubt and fear with positive and direct action. You cannot let fear hold you back.

> **"Courage is resistance to fear, mastery of fear, not absence of fear."** Mark Twain

What to do if you start to lose confidence:

1). Identify the root cause: It is easy for people to feel unconfident when they don't know exactly why they feel this way. But successful people know to search for the root cause by asking questions, such as when did I recognize my confidence was jarred? What was I doing when I noticed my confidence waning? Is this a cognitive distortion (all-or-nothing, black-and-white thinking)?

2). Resist conformity: Conformity leads to losing yourself and your confidence. Successful people need to have the ability to resist conformity. Remember that you're a leader, not a follower. Though we all have the desire to fit in, you shouldn't try to at the cost of losing confidence and who you are at your core.

3). Continually build confidence: It takes hard work to achieve great things, so building confidence in yourself must become part of your everyday life. Make it a daily habit to take inventory on your thought patterns. Become more aware of the negative messages you tell yourself, promptly challenge them, and replace it all with positive dialogue.

"I was always looking outside myself for strength and confidence, but it comes from within. It is there all the time." Anna Freud

Confidence helps you perform better, be relaxed, chase your dreams by setting goals, take risks, remove fear and doubt, and challenge negative thought patterns. Successful people know confidence leads to bigger and better things. Confidence sets the stage for success. Do you have confidence in yourself?

CALM IN A CRISIS

Being successful can also come with high stress and highly volatile situations. Successful people don't fall apart or lose their cool in a crisis. Successful people have learned how to stay calm when others are losing their heads around them. Despite the pressure, they maintain a positive mental attitude. They recognize the challenge as an opportunity rather than a dire threat.

"Crises are part of life. Everybody has to face them, and it doesn't make any difference what the crisis is." Jack Nicklaus

Successful people know that freaking out is not an option. Moreover, it paints a person in a very bad light and suggests they cannot handle the responsibility of their role. Successful people focus on the problem not the emotions swirling around the crisis. They do not take on the emotions of the people caught up in the crisis.

"Any kind of crisis can be good. It wakes you up." Ryan Reynolds

Communication is always key, but during a crisis calm, concise, and directive communication is a must.

Remember, your body language and facial expressions represent 70-90% of the message you're trying to convey. This is another time when your physical appearance will dictate how your message is received.

> **"Faced with crisis, the man of character falls back on himself. He imposes his own stamp of action, takes responsibility for it, makes it his own."** Charles de Gaulle

During a crisis, if another person is about to lose control or has lost control, successful people take a break and come back when tempers are calm. They remove themself from the situation to allow the other person to de-escalate. Successful people know it's easier to stay calm when they remind themself that they cannot control everything. Therefore, successful people don't worry about things they cannot control, but they do take immediate action on the things they can.

> **"Don't wait until you're in a crisis to come up with a crisis plan."** Dr. Phil

During a crisis, remember to be aware of your breathing. Breathing is essential. Take long-deep breaths. Exhale slowly. Successful people often utilize box breathing. What is box breathing? Box breathing, or what is also known as four-square breathing, is used to calm the mind while taking slow, deep breaths. It can improve performance and concentration while also reducing stress. It's a perfect breathing tool if you're feeling like you're stressed or losing your calm.

How to box breath:

1). Slowly inhale through your nose as you count to four and concentrate on the air filling your lungs.

2). Hold your breath counting to four.

3). Slowly exhale out from your mouth counting to four.

4). Repeat four times or until you're calm.

"Close scrutiny will show that most 'crisis situations' are opportunities to either advance or stay where you are." Maxwell Maltz

Successful people maintain a positive mental attitude during crisis. They recognize challenges as opportunities; focus on the problem not emotions; utilize calm, concise, and directive communication; project positive nonverbal cues; remove themselves if tempers get heated; and utilize breathing techniques to remain calm. How are you in a crisis?

SELF-DETERMINATION

Successful people are self-determined individuals. Self-determination refers to the ability one has to make choices and manage one's own life. A self-determined person is not one to sit around waiting for others to lead and manage them. Self-determined people and their behaviors tend to be intrinsically motivated and driven by enjoyment, interest, and innate satisfaction. Money is not their primary motivator.

"Freedom is self-determination." Baruch Spinoza

Self-determined people navigate their career and lives in the direction they want them to go. They have the power to decide who they want to be and what they want to do in life gives them a great deal of satisfaction and empowerment. They are resilient and eager to find their own path and do not rely on external motivation or direction.

> **If you are not willing to learn, no one can help you. If you are determined to learn, no one can stop you.**

Self-determination also sets them apart from others and encourages them to be strong and capable throughout life - making them a highly valuable individual to others. The ability to tackle a crisis quickly and confidently gives self-determined people a strong sense of self-awareness, enabling them to serve as a reliable leader for others around them.

> **"Be determined to handle any challenge in a way that will make you grow."** Les Brown

Self-determined individuals thrive on autonomy. In order to feel self-determined, people need to feel like they can take direct action to affect real change. This sense of control plays a major role in helping them feel confident. This is why so many self-determined people work for themselves. They truly feel the need to be the captain of their own ships.

> **"Self-determination is not a mere phrase. It is an imperative principle of action, which statesmen will henceforth ignore at their peril."**
> Woodrow Wilson

Those who are self-determined are competent to stand on their own and do so often. Self-determined people have the skills needed for success in their area of expertise and are more likely to take actions that will help them succeed. The more skills a person has, not surprisingly, the more likely they will use them to assert themselves and accomplish their goals.

"Success is no accident. It is hard work, perseverance, learning, studying, sacrifice, and most of all, love what you are doing." Pelé

Though self-determined people are focused on self, it does not mean they do not value connectedness to others. Self-determined people need to feel a sense of belonging and are known to have healthy attachments (emotional bonds with others). Self-determined people are proficient leaders who are great motivators of others, but equally work well alone.

"It is not the strongest species that survive, nor the most intelligent, but the ones most responsive to change." Charles Darwin

Self-determined people are motivated, empowered, resilient, self-aware, and confident reliable leaders. They navigate their own careers and can handle crisis. They thrive on autonomy; are competent and action-oriented; and have a sense of belonging. They are responsive to change. Are you living a self-determined life?

STORYTELLER

Successful people are great storytellers. They know who their audience is, and they home in on their target. They know exactly what message they want to convey before they say word number one. They understand their story must have a moral that is compelling, and they know exactly how to illustrate it with their words.

> **"Storytelling is the most powerful way to put ideas into the world today."** Robert McKee

Great storytellers tell stories that involve them, and therefore, they are deeply connected and passionate about them. They know how to be part of the story, but quite often they are not the hero. They are most often the person who has learned a life lesson the hard way so that others will avoid their fate. Moreover, if they can tell a story that the listener sees themselves in and can connect to, it is all the more powerful.

> **"Marketing is no longer about the stuff that you make, but about the stories you tell."** Seth Godin

Like a great book or movie, there is often a struggle. Conflict engages people and moves the story forward.

This is where the challenge escalates, and the stakes are raised. Storytellers get people on the edge of their seats to live the tale. Without a literal call to arms, the story itself motivates the listener to join the storyteller in the journey.

> **"Stories create community, enable us to see through the eyes of other people, and open us to the claims of others."** Peter Forbes

Successful storytellers say just enough and let the listener fill in their own details. This allows the listener to be an active participant and uses their imagination to further connect them to the story. Telling a great story doesn't happen overnight. It's much like doing stand-up. You practice your bit over and over again until it is well-crafted.

> **"Sometimes reality is too complex. Stories give it form."** Jean Luc Godard

Successful people and history show that words can change the world. What story will you share to motivate others?

ADD VALUE

In order to add value to someone, one must recognize what they value, and what their personal vision is for themselves. Then help make it a reality. To add value to others means to be intentional about serving others. For that to happen, it has to enrich the lives of others and enhance their quality of life. It's not simply for the benefit of yourself or the organization, but to improve the quality of the individuals' lives. If you can do this, your team will view you as a compassionate and inspired leader.

> **"If your Idea cannot change the industry, you have added no value."** Fela Durotoye

When trying to add value, always remember to ask, "Who is my audience?" It's surprising to think that anyone would attempt to be successful in business and start a business venture without ever asking, "Is there a need? Who is my audience? Do they need my product or service? Does this product or service best serve those in need?" In reality, this often-fatal misstep happens day in and day out.

> **"We get paid by bringing value to the marketplace."** Jim Rohn

Successful people have already asked these important questions, including who their audience is and how do they serve them. They maintain a deep understanding of the value they offer their audience and what value they can add to them.

> **"Little did I realize that my desire to add value to others would be the thing that added value to me!"** John C. Maxwell

They make it a habit to ask questions rather than make assumptions. They believe whole-heartedly in their product or service and are driven by the value it adds - not the dollars it generates. Money is not the most valuable measure to successful people. It's the value their creation adds to their audience.

> **"I measure my success in life by the added value my presence brought to those whom I loved, and who loved me."** R. A. Salvatore

This process of determining what value you can add to your audience can be applied to management as well. Successful leaders are able to recognize how they can help their team by asking questions, such as "How can I show them true leadership? Do they generally desire my help or need my help? How can I offer meaningful assistance, training, or mentoring? How do I instill trust in my team?"

"My mission is to add value. My attitude is of active curiosity and my method is through relationships of trust." Francois Baird

Teams appreciate and are motivated by leaders who serve their needs in a way that adds value to them as team members. Successful people know they add real value, as it is often knowledge, skills, and knowhow that their team will carry with them into the future.

"People who add value to others do so intentionally. I say that because to add value, leaders must give of themselves, and that rarely occurs by accident." John C. Maxwell

Successful people make it a habit to understand and value other people. They improve the lives of others by asking what their audience needs. They look for opportunities to better serve them. They believe wholeheartedly in their product and services. They instill trust and belief in their consumers or team by adding unique value to their lives. And isn't that what it's all about? How do you add value to others?

DAILY TASK RECORD

Successful people make it a habit to start off every morning by writing a list of tasks (in their journal or on note cards) that they have to get done for the day. Then, they check them off one by one, making sure they complete them all before they call it a day. Notice, it says "have to get done," not a "maybe get done" list. Successful people are action-driven and task-focused, and they accomplish what they set out to do.

"Accountability breeds response-ability."
Stephen R. Covey

Additionally, most successful people are accustomed to keeping a journal of their activities so that they can track their daily achievements. This is also why they have a habit of getting things done on time. Most people find a paper and pen to be all they need to stay on track, but there are countless apps and programs to utilize for managing daily tasks. Use whatever is easiest for you so that you don't skip an important note or deadline.

"What you get by achieving your goals is not as important as what you become by achieving your goals." Henry David Thoreau

Task records help people stay organized and follow through on important tasks. It is easier to focus by breaking down tasks. Lists hold you accountable. Writing it down helps imprint it in your mind, but it also holds you accountable. Lists draw on our desire to cross things off or put a check next to it as an accomplishment. Progress reduces stress and keeps your mind focused on the positive: that you're making progress.

> **"Accountability is the measure of a leaders height."** Jeffrey Benjamin

Lists provide a great visual aid to see what we have on our schedule, and lists allow a person to squeeze in or fit in additional tasks. Instead of trying to guess if you have enough time to take on or complete a task, you can see your schedule and prioritize what needs to be accomplished next. Though the goal is to complete every task…every day, at times, it simply is not possible when a crisis arises. The list is a perfect reference to also remind yourself that you may need to delegate specific tasks to your team.

> **"At the end of the day we are accountable to ourselves - our success is a result of what we do."** Catherine Pulsifer

Overall, a daily task record is a simple tool for organizing your day, tracking achievements, following through on tasks, holding yourself accountable, providing flexibility, prioritizing tasks, never forgetting things, reducing stress, and improving efficiency. Remember, don't forget to schedule time for exercise, friends and family, and reading. It's all about balance! What does your daily task record look like? If you're not using one, why not?

THE 80/20 RULE

Successful people utilize the 80/20 rule. What is the 80/20 rule? Known as the Pareto Principle, the 80/20 rule was developed in 1895 by the Italian economist Vilfredo Pareto. According to him, society was naturally divided into the "vital few," which is to say, those with money and influence (the 20 percent), and the "trivial many," which is to say, the 80 percent who had nothing.

Based on Pareto's analysis of various industries, he found that 80% of production was usually derived from just 20% of companies. The generalization is that 80% of results should come from just 20% of the actions. This has been applied to sales too. Therefore, it is believed that 80% of revenue comes from 20% of a company's clients.

Give it a try, and you will be amazed how many things in your life break down into the 80/20 rule. Successful people use this rule as they understand 80% of their revenue comes from 20% of their clients. Therefore, those are their target clients. Twenty percent of their products generate 80% of their revenue. This information is critical information.

"In business the 80/20 principle is behind any innovation, any extra value. It is an entrepreneurial principle, a formula for value creation utilized not only by entrepreneurs, but by most managers and organizations."
Richard Koch

Think of a restaurant when they realize that out of 100 items on their menu, 20 of those items generate 80% of their business. By knowing this, they can lower inventory and reduce offerings to become more streamlined and more profitable. Think about the clothes in your closet. Most men will wear 20% of their items 80% of the time. Think about the time and money wasted searching through unworn clothing 365 days a year. I'd bet 20% of the people in your phone list that you communicate with equal 80% of your total communications. Check it out for yourself.

The 80/20 rule allows successful people to focus on who and what drives their business, allowing those who use it to cut down on focusing on the wrong things. It affords those who use it more time to focus on key aspects of their business, and isn't that what really matters? Have you ever used the 80/20 rule?

REMOVE ADDICTION

If you want to be successful and remain successful, forgoing addiction and removing it from your life is an absolute. Successful people know addiction can rob them of their creativity, focus, quality of life/health, and of their existence. Think of how many beautiful and talented people who have lost battles with addiction. The list of talented musicians and artists alone would fill this entire book. Make no mistake, addiction destroys lives.

> **"First you take a drink, then the drink takes a drink, then the drink takes you."**
> F. Scott Fitzgerald

According to the CDC in 2019, "an estimated 95,000 Americans die of alcohol-related causes every year (approximately 68,000 men and 27,000 women)." Alcohol is the third most preventable cause of death in the United States. The latest CDC statistics reported that "In 2019, 70,630 drug overdose deaths occurred in the United States. The age-adjusted rate of overdose deaths increased by over 4% from 2018 (20.7 per 100,000) to 2019 (21.6 per 100,000) and is the number one leading cause of injury-related deaths."

A substance use disorder occurs when a substance is uncontrollably used despite harmful consequences. Those with substance use disorders have an intense focus on using a substance, such as alcohol or drugs, to the point where they are unable to function normally in day-to-day life. It is common for people to keep using substances even when they are aware of the consequences. This is a mental health issue.

Alcohol and Drug Health Issues (partial list):

Pancytopenia: Alcohol depletes the bone marrow of its white blood cells, red blood cells, and platelets.

Cardiovascular symptoms: Cardiomyopathy is caused by alcohol, essentially turning the heart muscle into mush. Drinking alcohol can also cause congestive heart failure by decreasing ejection fraction.

Cancer: As a result of alcohol consumption, there is an increased risk of cancer, particularly esophageal, liver, mouth, throat, and colorectal cancers.

Dementia: The effects of mind-altering substances like alcohol on the brain are not surprising. Alcohol dementia is a very real thing, and new technology is letting us distinguish between alcohol dementia and Alzheimer's.

Immune suppression: Alcohol consumption makes you more susceptible to infections.

Stroke: People who use drugs and alcohol are at greater risk of both hemorrhagic and ischemic strokes.

"Recovery is something that you have to work on every single day and it's something that doesn't get a day off." Demi Lovato

Stages of Recovery:

Precontemplation: In this stage, you may not accept that you have a problem. You may even defend your drug or alcohol use.

Contemplation: You start to understand the significance of people expressing concern for your welfare in this stage. You start to consider the effects that your substance use disorder may have on your body, as well as the negative effect it can have on the relationships in your life.

Preparation: When you figure out that the burden you carry does not deserve your time or attention, you accept the facts before you. As a result, you move past this stage.

Action: When you achieve this stage, you begin to believe that you can make a change for the better. Making this decision is a huge step that moves you forward in a huge way.

Maintenance: Once you are successful at avoiding temptations that lead you back to your old habits, you reach this stage in addiction recovery.

"Rock bottom became the solid foundation on which I rebuilt my life." J.K. Rowling

If you want to be successful, you must overcome addiction and remove it from your life. Too many successful people fall victim to their addictions, and it robs them of their talent and their life. Remember, alcohol and drug use are debts unpaid. At this moment, you may not believe you are suffering the consequences of addiction; but the damage is being done, and the bill will eventually come due. Successful people know when to get help. If you're struggling with addiction, please contact **SAMHSA's National Helpline 1-800-662-HELP**. You can overcome your addiction.

ASK QUESTIONS

We all started out in life asking question upon question. It's how we have learned to understand and navigate the world. A successful person knows they can solve problems by utilizing their networks. Where others are either afraid or embarrassed to ask questions, successful people are open to finding the answers they need by asking others for their expert advice. They don't hesitate to email or call the best person to answer their questions. In fact, they prepare the right questions in advance and are willing to help others in return.

"It is not the answer that enlightens, but the question." Eugene Ionesco

Why then, outside of fear, are questions avoided despite how invaluable they can be? Some people avoid questions because they are egocentric and do not believe they can learn from others. Some people assume they already know the answers and are overconfident. Both reasons do not serve the overall goal, which is to find the answer to a question. In comparison, successful people have solid ego strength and realize they simply cannot know every answer. They are willing to ask questions to serve the greater good.

"The only true wisdom is in knowing that you know nothing." Socrates

In order to be successful, not only do you need to utilize your network and ask questions, but you must get in the habit to ask the right questions. There are key areas to focus on in order to ask the best questions.

Clarification and follow up questions: Sometimes asking just one question isn't enough. At times, answers can be complex, and you need clarification; maybe you realized you didn't phrase your question correctly or even ask the right question to begin with.

Tone: Be mindful of your tone and body language. How you ask sets the tone of the conversation too. People can be taken back if they feel you are interrogating them rather than asking them a question. It's beneficial to start with an explanation of why you're asking the question. Remember to not hit someone over the head with your question or come out of left field with it. Make it a habit to monitor your tone.

Listen: It sounds simple enough, but you've asked your question, and now it's time to give the person time to answer your question. Do not interrupt them, as it's disrespectful and can give the impression you don't really value what they have to say. Actively listen and then follow up with clarification or another question.

Thank the person: Again, a very simple way to show that you appreciate and value someone and the time they have given you is to simply say please and thank you. They are fundamental in communication.

"The best scientists and explorers have the attributes of kids! They ask questions and have a sense of wonder. They have curiosity. 'Who, what, where, why, when and how!' They never stop asking questions, and I never stop asking questions, just like a five-year-old." Sylvia Earle

Successful people make it a habit to not let the fear of embarrassment, ego, or narcissism get in the way of asking questions. They take the time to formulate their question as to not waste their time or others. They're mindful of their tone. They make sure not to come across as interrogating. They listen to responses. They ask clarifying and appropriate follow up questions; and they show gratitude and thanks to others for their assistance. How are you at asking questions?

SACRIFICE

Starting out, the successful people will give up a substantial part of their income, drive a more affordable car, and rent an affordable place or downsize their home. They invest or reinvest the money they save into something that will generate more income in the future. Frugality is more important to the successful person's goals than splurging on expensive clothing, cars, a home, or superfluous possessions. Successful people invest in their future and growth.

> **"The most important decision about your goals is not what you're willing to do to achieve them, but what you are willing to give up."**
> Dave Ramsey

Time is our most valuable commodity, and successful people invest that time into themselves and their future. They maximize every hour of their day. This is not to say they don't relax, take breaks, exercise, and spend time with friends and family - because they do. But what they don't do is waste time. They sacrifice free time to further invest in reading, research, education, investments, business plans, and startups to name a few.

Successful people sacrifice stability of a 9-5 job for entrepreneurship, working at a fast-paced startup, or building a partnership with others. Yes, it's nice to have steady income or set hours, but successful people know that their long-term goals will provide more opportunity in the long run.

> **"The speed of your success is limited only by your dedication and what you're willing to sacrifice."** Nathan W. Morris

Successful people make it a habit to stick to their action plans and will not compromise their future by losing progress on their goals. They often sacrifice free time by having to work long days, nights, weekends and holidays. They tend to have less opportunity for sleep.

When it's all said and done, successful people make it a habit to put off many of the immediate desires that others indulge in daily. They fight the urge and make a conscious choice to not to take it easy, procrastinate, or waste time. They forgo utilizing social media except to launch business ventures and brands, watching television, and even going on dates (for a period of time).

> **"Are you ready to sacrifice who you are, for what you will become."** Eric Thomas

Successful people sacrifice luxury items and time. They invest in their education and future. They work instead of procrastinating or taking it easy, and they forgo immediate desires. Are they crazy? Ask Warren Buffett. He stated he never spends more than $4 a day for breakfast, and he's one of the wealthiest and most successful individuals on the planet.

Frugality and sacrifice are not just for those starting out, but a way of life too. To successful people, it's almost always more important what they can do from their sacrifices, than about what they can't do. What sacrifices can you implement to improve your life and become more successful?

REINVENTION

Reinventing yourself isn't easy; however, learning new skills and adapting to new situations are essential for professional and personal success. As we move through life, our ability to adapt, evolve, develop skills, and embrace change determines how much success we will achieve inside and outside the workplace. Successful people make it a habit to reinvent themselves when necessary.

> **"People who cannot invent and reinvent themselves must be content with borrowed postures, secondhand ideas, fitting in instead of standing out."** Warren Bennis

Many successful individuals have reinvented themselves several times throughout their lives. Dwayne "The Rock" Johnson went from college football player to wrestler to actor to film producer. Elon Musk went from PayPal to Tesla to SpaceX. Robert Downey Jr. went from being an unhirable actor to leading a Marvel franchise. Angelina Jolie went from actress to director to United Nations Ambassador. Arnold Schwarzenegger went from body builder to actor to politician - and back to actor. George Foreman went from boxer to brand ambassador.

"When I let go of what I am, I become what I might be." Lao Tzu

With rapidly changing technological, economic, and political environments around the world, the world has become an unpredictable place. Industries are transforming, and work is going through a revolution. In order to stay relevant, you need to be able to reinvent yourself on a continual basis. Changing things up is more than just survival. If life becomes too familiar, creative and successful people become bored and restless. Successful people need change to challenge themselves and keep their lives interesting.

The psychological challenge of reinventing oneself is considerable. First of all, we are short-term thinkers. Research has demonstrated that we often opt for immediate rewards over later ones, even if they are greater. Successful people make it a habit to acknowledge the "Id" need for instant gratification and balance their decision with the "Ego," which is focused on mediating reality.

There are many ways to reinvent yourself, but I found that becoming my alter ego was key to my reinvention. I took the best parts of both real and fictional characters and made a list of positive attributes I had to incorporate. I chose James Bond (minus the killing) meets Frank

Abignale (*Catch Me if You Can*) and P.T. Barnum (minus overhyping but rather overachieving what is promised).

> **"You never change things by fighting the existing reality. To change something, build a new model that makes the existing model obsolete."** R. Buckminster Fuller

I dressed the part, learned the roles expected of me, and incorporated the strength of these individuals to overthrow my insecurities. I did not become a caricature of myself. I became the reinvention of the perfect parts of my alter-egos. I became a talent agent, Grammy member, author, public speaker, and more. It's something my younger self would have never imagined. As my alter-ego, I am unstoppable. Through habit, I have become more than the sum of my parts, and I am the best version of me. And I will continue to reinvent and grow.

In addition to professional and personal success, survival, opportunity, changing things up to not become complacent and bored, and reinventing yourself to live more in alignment with your goals, you can transform your life satisfaction. Studies have shown that a midlife career shift can enhance brain cognition, well-being, and longevity too. Is it time for you to reinvent yourself?

CURIOSITY

From an early age we are lined up in neat rows, told to sit up straight, face forward, and basically follow the leader. But people who are successful see the world through different lenses. They're naturally curious and question everything. Successful people begin with "why?" They break down problems like machinery to see what went wrong and how to solve a problem. They are curious about why and how things work, and in what ways things can be changed.

"Curiosity is the engine of achievement."
Sir Ken Robinson

Successful people don't accept the status quo, and they aren't afraid of challenging conventional wisdom. They have a curious and inquisitive mind, which leads them to make new discoveries and change the way things are done. There are benefits to being curious aside from the knowledge one gains. Curiosity benefits success by:

1). You succeed when you are curious, because when you are curious, you are more interesting and more intelligent. You ask questions. You learn more. Your curiosity will be interpreted by others as intelligence and increase your potential for opportunities.

2). Research indicates that when you are curious, the limbic reward system of the brain is active. The limbic system is the part of the brain involved in our behavioral and emotional responses, especially when it comes to behaviors we need for memory. Curious people often learn best this way and have great memory - even as they age.

"Curiosity is the hunger of the human mind."
Rose Wilder Lane

3). Entrepreneurs and successful people have an ongoing need to send the right message. It is important to convey the message that you prefer asking questions over pretending to know all the answers. Asking questions shows humility too which is a great way to come across to your audience.

4). Curious people tend to have better social networks because they are knowledgeable about a variety of subjects and capable of carrying on meaningful conversation. To ask questions is to learn, and to learn is the ability to share that learned information with others. Curiosity has a profound impact on how we grow and how we develop relationships with others. Curious people are usually passionate people, and who doesn't like to spend time with a curious and passionate person?

"Ideas come from curiosity." Walt Disney

Successful people make it a habit to understand how things work. They challenge conventional wisdom and the status quo. They are more interesting and knowledgeable (which attracts others to them), and they are humble, passionate, and great at cultivating relationships through asking questions and sharing knowledge with others. What are you curious about?

TAKE ACTION

There's an old saying, "The best time to plant a tree was 20 years ago. The second-best time is today." If you wait for the perfect moment, you will be waiting forever. There's no such thing as the perfect moment.

Every year, it is reported 50% of people wait until New Year's Day to make a resolution and take action. Within two weeks, 80-90% have already given up on that action. Waiting to take action has no statistical benefit. Moreover, taking action due to feeling pressure to do so - or when you're not emotionally connected to the goal - is a failure in the making.

> **"Do you want to know who you are? Don't ask. Act! Action will delineate and define you."**
> Thomas Jefferson

Successful people determine what goal they need to take action on and believe in their goal. Whether they set personal goals or business goals, they clearly define what the problem is that requires setting a plan into action. They anticipate obstacles, including environmental, financial, emotional, and physical barriers to change.

They take immediate action to form a plan, but they don't act impulsively or recklessly. They take immediate action with logical steps that include formulating a plan, but they don't procrastinate on creating a plan or make excuses why they can't create a plan now.

> **"Be content to act and leave the talking to others."** Baltasar Gracian

Identifying a plan of action is a great start. Successful people make it a habit to take a moment and identify which actions can lead to success rather than wasting time taking impulsive steps that can lead them to failure. In other words, make sure that you are prioritizing the right action plan before you start taking misguided steps in the wrong direction.

Starting from a place where you know there is no perfect time, allows you to have an open mind and recognize there is not always going to be a perfect outcome to your action.

Successful people are prepared to hit barriers and face setbacks - but knowing this ahead of time gives them the fortitude to accept that no plan is foolproof and that adjustments may need to be made. Having a flexible mindset allows successful people to misstep, but not face utter failure. Acceptance and adaptation are key when taking immediate action.

"Inaction breeds doubt and fear. Action breeds confidence and courage. If you want to conquer fear, do not sit home and think about it. Go out and get busy." Dale Carnegie

Anyone can come up with an excuse why they should not take action. The lists of why nots can go on for infinity. There's never going to be a shortage of excuses in the world, and without trying very hard, you can find many. Successful people know that every excuse leads to procrastination, and that's where dreams and goals die a slow death. Successful people find reasons why they should take action to improve their life and achieve their goals - not why they should wait until the perfect time. Are you ready to take action?

NARRATIVE

René Descartes said, "I think therefore I am." Nothing could be truer when it comes to our narrative. The stories we tell ourselves become our reality. Successful people know our stories influence every ounce of our identities, aspirations, and experiences, as well as set the boundaries for what we can achieve (or not achieve). Therefore, narratives are heavily influenced by internal dialogue, but they are also influenced by external sources. Both have immense power to elevate a person or destroy their potential.

> **"After food, shelter, and companionship, stories are the thing we need most in the world."**
> Philip Pullman

Take a child like myself who was raised being called a "moron" and an "idiot." They begin to believe they are those things. They question whether they are smart enough in school. Before long, they believe they are not smart enough. Instead of asking questions, the external dialogue soon takes over their internal dialogue, and they take ownership that they are a "moron" and an "idiot" - incapable of getting the correct answers. They shut down. They accept the external narrative and begin to fulfill it.

Successful people have learned that they need to destroy these negative self-images, not accept ownership of external and false narratives, and control their own lives through their true narrative. They make a conscious effort to stop allowing the negative feedback loops to play in their heads, including the negative self-talk. They make a conscious effort to disrupt the negative flow of dialogue replacing it with their own positive and realistic narrative that is filled with hope, opportunity, and growth.

> **"When I am afraid to speak is when I speak.
> That is when it is most important."**
> Nayyirah Waheed

Successful people make it a habit to create their own vision of who they are and who they want to be. They pay particular attention to the things they can control in their life, such as their own actions, thoughts, attitude, internal dialogue, and how they define their self. They become receptive to feedback but are quick to filter out unrealistic and unhealthy dialogue directed at them. They no longer take ownership of demoralizing and untrue statements about who they are or what they are capable of.

Equally important, they take positive action. They now have control of their mental state. They break out of the box of negativity and accept challenges, take risks, and make progress toward their goals - redefining what it means to be them. They fully understand how detrimental their internal dialogue is to control a healthy and success-driven narrative. Now, take daily action toward sculpting the narrative they desire and deserve.

> **"Owning our story and loving ourselves through that process is the bravest thing that we will ever do."** Brené Brown

Successful people recognize narratives shape their identities, aspirations, and experiences. They do not let false and negative external dialogue shape who they are. They destroy negative images and do not accept ownership of false narratives. Success comes from taking control of your thoughts and actions, and living your own narrative based on your goals. Successful people live their narrative under their own terms, and so should you. Are you in control of your own narrative today?

> **"Sometimes, all you need are the right words at the right time to change how you see the world...including yourself."** Shawn Léon Nowotnik

NOTES

Habits

Clear, J. (2021, March 9). *The habits guide: How to build good habits and break bad ones.* https://jamesclear.com/habits.

Habits shape your life! (n.d.). https://www.theworldcounts.com/happiness/psychology-of-habits.

Time it Takes for a Habit

Grohol, J. (2018). *Need to form a new habit? Give yourself at least 66 days.* https://psychcentral.com/blog/need-to-form-a-new-habit-66-days.

Lally, P., Jaarsveld, C. H. M. van, Potts, H. W. W., & Wardle, J. (2009, July 16). How are habits formed: Modelling habit formation in the real world. *Wiley Online Library.* https://onlinelibrary.wiley.com/doi/abs/10.1002/ejsp.674.

How long does it take to form a habit? (2018). https://www.ucl.ac.uk/news/2009/aug/how-long-does-it-take-form-habit.

SMART Goals

Traugott, J. (2021, January 13). *Achieving your goals: An evidence-based approach.* MSU Extension. https://www.canr.msu.edu/news/achieving_your_goals_an_evidence_based_approach.

Smart goals: How to make your goals achievable. (n.d). https://www.mindtools.com/pages/article/smart-goals.htm.

Exercise and Health

7 great reasons why exercise matters. (n.d.) Mayo Foundation for Medical Education and Research. https://www.mayoclinic.org/healthy-lifestyle/fitness/in-depth/exercise/art-20048389.

Nutrition

Welcome. (n.d.) https://www.nutrition.gov/.

Healthy Diet. (n.d.) World Health Organization. https://www.who.int/news-room/fact-sheets/detail/healthy-diet.

CDC. (2021). *Healthy eating for a healthy weight.* https://www.cdc.gov/healthyweight/healthy_eating/index.html.

Start Early

Is waking up early good or bad? (n.d.) BBC Worklife. BBC. https://www.bbc.com/worklife/article/20190213-is-waking-up-early-good-or-bad.

Yates, E. (2017). *A Navy SEAL commander explains why you should make your bed every single day. Business Insider.*

https://www.businessinsider.com/navy-seal-commander-explains-why-you-should-make-your-bed-2017-4.

Focused Thinking

Schön, N. (2021, October 13). *Focused vs. diffuse thinking: Which is better for learning?* Brainscape Academy. https://www.brainscape.com/academy/focused-vs-diffuse-thinking-learning/.

Networking with Like Minds

Augustine, A. (2021, November 19). *Here's why networking is important to your success.* TopResume. https://www.topresume.com/career-advice/importance-of-networking-for-career-success.

Caramba, N. (2017, October 24). *How to acquire like-minded people in your network and increase your chances of success.* Addicted 2 Success. https://addicted2success.com/success-advice/how-to-acquire-like-minded-people-in-your-network-and-increase-your-chances-of-success/.

Self-control

Self-control. (n.d.) Psychology Today. Accessed https://www.psychologytoday.com/us/basics/self-control.

Solution Focused

GoodTherapy Editor. (2018). *Solution-Focused Brief Therapy (SFBT).* https://www.goodtherapy.org/learn-about-therapy/types/solution-focused-therapy.

Partializing

Social Work Skills. (n.d). https://www.ssw.umaryland.edu/media/ssw/field-education/Social_Work_Skills.pdf.

Ziskin, L., & Schulman, T. (1991). *What about Bob?* United States; Buena Vista Pictures Distribution, Inc.

Gratitude

Economy, P. (2016). *14 scientifically proven ways gratitude can bring you success and happiness.* https://www.inc.com/peter-economy/14-powerfully-beneficial-effects-of-gratitude.html.

Meditation

Thorpe, M. (2020). *12 benefits of meditation.* Healthline. https://www.healthline.com/nutrition/12-benefits-of-meditation.

U.S. Department of Health and Human Services. (n.d.) *Meditation: In Depth.* National Center for Complementary and Integrative Health. https://www.nccih.nih.gov/health/meditation-in-depth.

Hickman, S., Corrigal, J. Miranda, G. and Brach, T. (n.d.). *How to meditate.* https://www.mindful.org/how-to-meditate/.

Humility

Orendorff, A. (2015). *Humility: The missing ingredient to your success.* Entrepreneur. https://www.entrepreneur.com/article/249412.

Accept Challenges

7 challenges successful people overcome. (n.d.) TalentSmart, https://www.talentsmarteq.com/articles/7-Challenges-Successful-People-Overcome-2147446608-p-1.html/.

Authentic Self

What it means to be your authentic self. (n.d.) Center for Growth Therapy. https://www.thecenterforgrowth.com/tips/what-it-means-to-be-your-authentic-self.

How to be your authentic self: 7 powerful strategies. (n.d.). SoulSalt, https://soulsalt.com/how-to-be-your-authentic-self/.

Emotional Intelligence

Why emotional intelligence makes you more successful. (2019). https://www.latrobe.edu.au/nest/why-emotional-intelligence-makes-you-more-successful/.

Improving emotional intelligence (EQ). (n.d.). HelpGuide.org, https://www.helpguide.org/articles/mental-health/emotional-intelligence-eq.htm.

Tredgold, G. (2016). *55 inspiring quotes that show the importance of emotional intelligence.* https://www.inc.com/gordon-tredgold/55-inspiring-quotes-that-show-the-importance-of-emotional-intelligence.html.

Journaling

7 benefits to keeping a journal. (2020). NW Health Blog, https://wa-health.kaiserpermanente.org/seven-journal-writing-benefits/.

Journaling for your health. (n.d.) Centers for Disease Control and Prevention. https://www.cdc.gov/diabetes/library/spotlights/journalinghealth.html

Smyth, J.M., Johnson, J., Auer, B., Lehman, E., Talamo, G., and Sciamanna, C. (2018). Online positive affect journaling in the improvement of mental distress and well-being in general medical patients with elevated anxiety symptoms: A preliminary randomized controlled trial." *JMIR mental health,* https://www.ncbi.nlm.nih.gov/pmc/articles/PMC6305886/.

Sleep

Walton, A. (2017). *The sleep habits of highly successful people.* Forbes Magazine,

190

https://www.forbes.com/sites/alicegwalton/2015/11/13/the-sleep-habits-of-highly-successful-people-infographic/?sh=36111e4b6d7f.

Ward, M. (2020). *15 things successful people do right before bed*. Business Insider. https://www.businessinsider.com/what-the-most-successful-people-do-right-before-bed-2015-2.

Therapy

Tartakovsky, M. (2019). *Benefits of therapy you probably didn't know about*. Psych central. https://psychcentral.com/blog/benefits-of-therapy-you-probably-didnt-know-about#3.

21 highly successful, inspiring people with mental health challenges. (2017). HealthyPsych.com, https://healthypsych.com/21-highly-successful-inspiring-people-with-mental-health-challenges/.

Psychotherapy. (2016). Mayo Foundation for Medical Education and Research. https://www.mayoclinic.org/tests-procedures/psychotherapy/about/pac-20384616.

7 steps to boost your self-esteem. (2020). Mayo Foundation for Medical Education and Research. https://www.mayoclinic.org/healthy-lifestyle/adult-health/in-depth/self-esteem/art-20045374.

Reading

Merle, A. (2017). *The reading habits of ultra-successful people*. HuffPost, https://www.huffpost.com/entry/the-reading-habits-of-ult_b_9688130.

Carlos, V. (2021). Why *reading is the habit of the highly successful*. Medium. https://medium.com/mind-cafe/why-reading-is-the-habit-of-the-highly-successful-7b8bd918b950.

Chon, M. (n.d.) *25 reading quotes that prove there's nothing in the world like a good book*. Oprah Daily. https://www.oprahdaily.com/life/g30000006/best-quotes-about-reading/?slide=8.

Time

deHaaff, B. (2016). *3 ways successful people manage their time*. https://www.inc.com/brian-de-haaff/3-ways-successful-people-manage-their-time.html.

Imafidon, C. (2015). *10 things successful people do to maximize their time*. Lifehack, https://www.lifehack.org/articles/productivity/10-things-successful-people-maximize-their-time.html.

They Accept failure

Allen, T. (2018). *3 things successful people do to leverage failure*. Forbes Magazine. https://www.forbes.com/sites/terinaallen/2018/11/16/successful-people-leverage-failure/?sh=4e21ffc672bc.

21 important lessons learned from failure. (n.d.). Wanderlust Worker, https://www.wanderlustworker.com/21-important-lessons-learned-from-failure/.

Chase their own Goals

Mahmood, U. (2015). *6 ways to start chasing your dreams.* Addicted 2
      Success. https://addicted2success.com/life/6-ways-to-start-chasing-
      your-dreams/.

Value Solitude

Morin, A. (2017). *7 science-backed reasons you should spend more time
      alone.* Forbes Magazine.
      https://www.forbes.com/sites/amymorin/2017/08/05/7-science-
      backed-reasons-you-should-spend-more-time-
      alone/?sh=194d646b1b7e.

Feedback

DeFranzo. (n.d.). *5 reasons why feedback is important.*
      https://www.snapsurveys.com/blog/5-reasons-feedback-important/.

Perseverance

Hoque, F. (2015). *What highly successful people know about perseverance.*
      Fast Company. https://www.fastcompany.com/3049327/lessons-
      highly-successful-have-learned-about-perseverance.
Muguku, D. (2018). *9 tips on how to persevere in order to succeed.*
      ThriveYard. https://www.thriveyard.com/9-tips-on-how-to-persevere-
      in-order-to-succeed/.
Chinese bamboo tree ft. Les Brown. (2018, August 2). YouTube.
      https://www.youtube.com/watch?v=JCBU1gONp9w.

Take Risks

Why taking risks is the key to success. (n.d.). Flash Pack.
      https://www.flashpack.com/us/careers/taking-risks-key-to-success/.

Attention to Detail

Cuncic, A. (2020, May 25). *Practicing active listening in your daily
      conversations.* Verywell Mind. https://www.verywellmind.com/what-is-
      active-listening-3024343.
What are some examples of attention to detail? (2021, November 19).
      https://traqq.com/blog/attention-to-detail-why-it-matters-at-work/.

Balanced Life

Sanfilippo, M. (n.d.). *How to improve your work-life balance.* Business News
      Daily. https://www.businessnewsdaily.com/5244-improve-work-life-
      balance-today.html.

Trust Your Gut

Vozza, S. (2020, July 10). *5 ways to get better at trusting your gut.* Fast
      Company. https://www.fastcompany.com/90526352/5-ways-to-get-
      better-at-trusting-your-gut.

Raypole, C. (2021, January 27). *Trust your gut: What it actually means.*
     Healthline. https://www.healthline.com/health/mental-health/trust-
     your-gut#causes.

Root Cause

Thomas, J. (2020, November 27). *A simple 5 step root cause analysis process
     for your business.* Toggl Blog. https://toggl.com/blog/root-cause-
     analysis.

Not Afraid to Succeed

Pietrangelo, A. (2020, September 30). *What is a fear of success?* Healthline.
     https://www.healthline.com/health/anxiety/fear-of-success#strategies.
Tulshyan, R., & Burey, J. (2021, November 22). *Stop telling women they have
     imposter syndrome.* Harvard Business Review.
     https://hbr.org/2021/02/stop-telling-women-they-have-imposter-
     syndrome.

Strong Communicator

7 communication skills every entrepreneur must master. (2014, November
     10). Entrepreneur. https://www.entrepreneur.com/article/239446.
Patel, D. (2018, September 4). *10 powerful attributes of insanely successful
     people.* Entrepreneur. https://www.entrepreneur.com/article/319058.
Sinek, S. (n.d.). How great leaders inspire action. TED. Retrieved December 8,
     2021, from
     https://www.ted.com/talks/simon_sinek_how_great_leaders_inspire_a
     ction?language=en.

Growth Mindset

Patel, D. (2018, February 13). *10 ways to develop a success-oriented mindset.*
     Entrepreneur. https://www.entrepreneur.com/article/308895.
Reeves, M. (2021, April 22). *What is the purpose of mentoring?*
     https://www.togetherplatform.com/blog/what-is-the-purpose-of-
     mentoring.
The role of failure in learning. (2021, October 13). Oxford Learning.
     https://www.oxfordlearning.com/the-role-of-failure-in-learning/.

Passion

Smith, J. (2014, May 13). *CEO explains why passion is the key to success.*
     Business Insider. https://www.businessinsider.com/ceo-explains-why-
     passion-is-key-to-success-2014-5.
Lim, S. (2019, December 3). *Why passion is important for success.* Stunning
     Motivation. https://stunningmotivation.com/why-passion-is-
     important/.

Ambition

Vozza, S. (2015, December 21). *Six habits of ambitious people.* Fast Company. https://www.fastcompany.com/3048722/six-habits-of-ambitious-people.

Optimism

Ruthumohnews. (2017, October 5). *Why you should be highly optimistic if you want to be successful.* CNBC. https://www.cnbc.com/2017/10/05/why-should-you-be-highly-optimistic-if-you-want-to-be-successful.html.

Scott, E. (2020, October 11). *The differences between optimists and pessimists.* Verywell Mind. https://www.verywellmind.com/the-benefits-of-optimism-3144811.

Cuncic, A. (2020, July 1). *Change your thoughts, reduce your social anxiety.* Verywell Mind. https://www.verywellmind.com/what-is-cognitive-restructuring-3024490.

Gratitude. (n.d.). Psychology Today. https://www.psychologytoday.com/us/basics/gratitude

Confidence

Garnett, L. (2019, October 14). *How successful people deal when they're feeling a lack of confidence.* Business Insider. https://www.businessinsider.com/3-ways-that-successful-people-deal-with-a-lack-of-confidence-10#strategy-3-they-make-confidence-building-a-habit-3.

Calm in a Crisis

Stinson, A. (2018, June 1). *Box breathing: How to do it, benefits, and tips.* Medical News Today. https://www.medicalnewstoday.com/articles/321805#the-box-breathing-method.

Burnett, J. (2021, July 13). *Six ways successful people stay calm in a crisis.* Ladders. https://www.theladders.com/career-advice/calm-anxiety-stress-crisis-insomnia.

Self-determination

Cherry, K. (2021, March 15). *How does self-determination theory explain motivation?* Verywell Mind. https://www.verywellmind.com/what-is-self-determination-theory-2795387.

Storyteller

O'Hara, C. (2015, August 12). *How to tell a great story.* Harvard Business Review. https://hbr.org/2014/07/how-to-tell-a-great-story.

Add Value

Maxwell, J. (2021, February 17). *Are you adding value to others? Developing a culture of leadership.* John Maxwell Company. https://corporatesolutions.johnmaxwell.com/blog/developing-a-culture-of-leadership-are-you-adding-value-to-others/.

Daily Task Record

Ho, L. (2019, December 18). *7 reasons why creating A to-do list makes you productive. Lifehack.* https://www.lifehack.org/859340/todo-list.

80/20 Rule

Kruse, K. (2016, March 8). *The 80/20 rule and how it can change your life.* Forbes. https://www.forbes.com/sites/kevinkruse/2016/03/07/80-20-rule/?sh=389d39f73814.

Remove Addiction

U.S. Department of Health and Human Services. (n.d.). *Alcohol Facts and Statistics.* National Institute on Alcohol Abuse and Alcoholism. https://www.niaaa.nih.gov/publications/brochures-and-fact-sheets/alcohol-facts-and-statistics.

Centers for Disease Control and Prevention. (2021, March 3). *Drug overdose deaths.* Centers for Disease Control and Prevention. https://www.cdc.gov/drugoverdose/deaths/index.html.

Behind the numbers: Alcohol Is Killing More... Caron Treatment Centers. (n.d.). https://www.caron.org/blog/alcohol-is-killing-more-people-than-the-opioid-epidemic.

National Institute on Drug Abuse. (2020, July 13). *Addiction and health.* National Institute on Drug Abuse. Retrieved December 3, 2021, from https://www.drugabuse.gov/publications/drugs-brains-behavior-science-addiction/addiction-health.

Berman, D. J. (2021, June 11). *What are the 5 stages of addiction recovery?* Discovery Institute. https://www.discoverynj.org/what-are-the-5-stages-of-addiction-recovery/.

Ask Questions

Tank, A. (2021, August 27). *The most successful people in the world ask questions constantly. here's how to master the art of asking questions.* Entrepreneur. https://www.entrepreneur.com/article/380818.

Sacrifice

Yau, T. (2021, March 2). *8 things successful people sacrifice for their success.* Lifehack. https://www.lifehack.org/articles/productivity/8-things-successful-people-sacrifice-for-their-success.html.

Reinvention

The power of reinventing yourself. IE Driving Innovation. (2020, September 16). https://drivinginnovation.ie.edu/the-power-of-reinventing-yourself/.

Ward, T. (2016, April 21). *Nine celebrities who have successfully reinvented their careers.* Forbes. https://www.forbes.com/sites/tomward/2016/04/21/nine-celebrities-who-have-successfully-reinvented-their-careers/?sh=36c6de8664dc.

Curiosity

Quy, L. R. (2019, August 23). *4 reasons why curiosity is critical to your success.* Ladders. https://www.theladders.com/career-advice/4-reasons-why-curiosity-is-critical-to-your-success.

Take Action

Murphy, M. (2020, February 11). *This is the month when New Year's resolutions fail-here's how to save them.* Forbes. https://www.forbes.com/sites/markmurphy/2020/02/11/this-is-the-month-when-new-years-resolutions-fail-heres-how-to-save-them/?sh=4de27333272f.

4 steps to take action on your goals. (2021, November 17). https://www.jackcanfield.com/blog/taking-action-on-our-goals/.

Narrative

Disrupt your own narrative. (2020, March 20). Harvard Business Review. https://hbr.org/2020/03/disrupt-your-own-narrative.

INDEX

W

Y

Z

NOTES

NOTES

NOTES

NOTES

ACKNOWLEDGEMENTS

First and foremost, this book would not have been possible without the inspiration and input I received from so many amazing and successful people, each of whom willingly gave me their time and wisdom. These individuals have all helped not only me, but countless others through their kindness.

To Mickie, for being my sounding board (once again) and instilling more urgency by telling me, "People... need this book." To the countless celebrities who have befriended me over the past two decades. To my publicist, Diane. To Karen Cadle for her kindness. To Teddy, who is always "off the hook."

To my family who has always been there for me, especially my mother who is always proud of me, my sister who encourages me to "chase my dreams," and to my brother who accepts me for "being me." To my cohort and colleagues who show unending support. To Dr. Calabria who keeps me healthy.

To my ex, who broke my heart, but not my spirit. You made me realize my roots needed to go down to Hell in order for me to be strong enough to grow and reach the heavens. To Richard Dreyfuss and Dr. Leo Marvin for introducing me to *Baby Steps*.

And you, for choosing to take steps toward changing your habits. As F. M. Alexander said, "People do not decide their futures, they decide their habits and their habits decide their futures." To your life, based on your healthy habits!

ABOUT THE AUTHOR

Shawn Léon Nowotnik, MSW, LCSW, is an artist, author, filmmaker, and therapist splitting his time between Chicago, IL and Los Angeles, CA. He understands firsthand how loss, mental health, and addiction can affect every aspect of a person's life, including their narrative. Shawn was forced to reevaluate his own narrative when he lost his son to suicide.

Today, Shawn focuses his energy on empowering others as an author and therapist, developing holistic treatment programs, advocating to improve how mental health and addiction disorders are treated, and researching and writing about social issues.

Shawn is available for public and private speaking engagements, keynote speeches, and panel discussions. A passionate and engaging presenter, Shawn speaks to topics focused in the areas of addiction, community, mental health, narrative, and social issues, and he offers personal insight into the greatest issues that face us as a society.

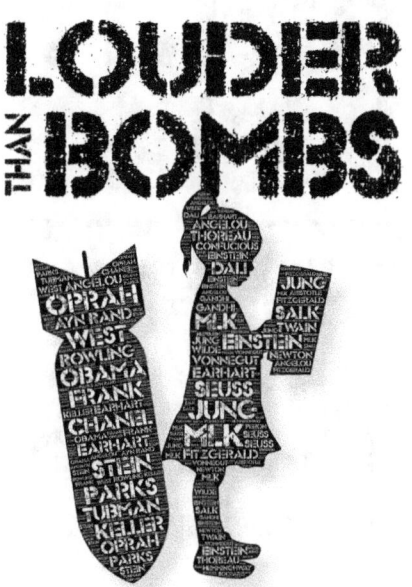

Louder Than Bombs is an incredible collection of motivating, inspiring, and self-affirming quotes that will challenge you to change your narrative. Discover a quote a day for inspiration or read it from cover-to-cover all at once. Through your journey, you will gain insights into becoming the person you were meant to be.

am-biv-a-lent

am-biv-a-lent.com

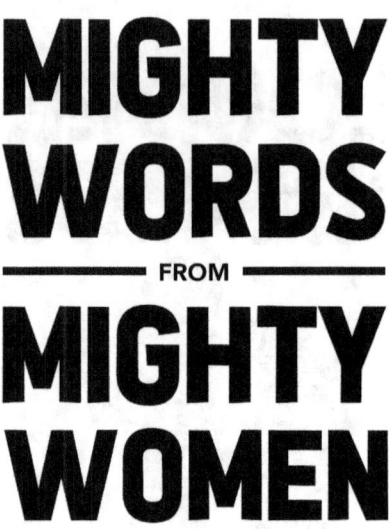

MIGHTY WORDS
— FROM —
MIGHTY WOMEN

Words That Will Inspire You

Mighty Words From Mighty Women is a collection of powerful, meaningful, and inspirational quotes from adventurers, artists, authors, civil rights activists, doctors, educators, humanitarians, inventors, orators, philosophers, poets, politicians, revolutionaries, scientists, and titans of industry. Everyone from Audrey Hepburn to Zendaya shares their words of hope, wisdom, and empowerment.

am-biv-a-lent

am-biv-a-lent.com

www.ingramcontent.com/pod-product-compliance
Lightning Source LLC
Chambersburg PA
CBHW060919120626
46553CB00001B/379